UNDERSTANDING ABUSE IN YOUNG PEOPLE'S INTIMATE RELATIONSHIPS

Female Perspectives on Power, Control and Gendered Social Norms

Ceryl Teleri Davies

P

First published in Great Britain in 2023 by

Policy Press, an imprint of
Bristol University Press
University of Bristol
1–9 Old Park Hill
Bristol
BS2 8BB
UK
t: +44 (0)117 374 6645
e: bup-info@bristol.ac.uk

Details of international sales and distribution partners are available at
policy.bristoluniversitypress.co.uk

British Library Cataloguing in Publication Data
A catalogue record for this book is available from the British Library

ISBN 978-1-4473-6266-1 hardcover
ISBN 978-1-4473-6267-8 paperback
ISBN 978-1-4473-6268-5 ePub
ISBN 978-1-4473-6269-2 ePdf

Cover design: Qube Design
Front cover image: iStock/Devonyu

Contents

List of tables

Acknowledgements

Hoffwn ddiolch i chwi o waelod fy ngalon!/I wish to thank you from the bottom of my heart!

This book would not be complete without special thanks to my family – you have all been wonderful! *Diolch mam a dad am bob dim*/Thanks to my mum and dad for everything! Thanks, Colin, for being a wonderful husband and father to our children and for supporting me throughout the process of writing this book. I sincerely thank my beautiful and wise children, Dafydd (Dafs) and Teleri (Tels). You are little lights that encourage me forward. I live to be your moral compass and beacon of support, and smile at the thought of your daily anecdotes and little words of wisdom. I do not underestimate how lucky I am to have both of you. I also have amazing, supportive friends; you know who you are! Special thanks go to my dear friends Elen, Gwen, Sam and Jo. I'm so fortunate to have been given this amazing opportunity, which has been life changing.

I owe sincere and warm thanks to both my wonderful PhD supervisors, Prof Sundari Anitha and Dr Ana Jordan. I would like to thank the University of Lincoln for funding this research, and for allowing me to pursue my aim of completing it in Wales, on a topic that impacts on the well-being of young women. I also give special thanks to my very patient and kind Welsh work colleagues, from the numerous local authorities that I have engaged with and also from Bangor University. Special thanks also go to Bangor University for continually supporting and promoting my work.

I also wish to thank Isobel Bainton and her colleagues at Policy Press, who guided me along the way to publication.

I would like to express my sincere gratitude to both local authorities and the seven schools who participated in this research. Finally, I warmly and respectfully thank the amazing young women who participated in all stages of this research – I learnt so much from working with you. This book would not have been possible without your honest and brave input throughout.

Introduction

Writing is a process that brings you closer to your own identity, if that makes sense! It makes you reflect on your own values, attitudes and experiences. The person you were, the person you have become and who you strive to be in the future. Writing this book has made me think back to my teenage years, times that were both joyful and painful in equal measure. One overwhelming reflection was the feeling that constant harassment, sexism and abuse continues to invade and shape the experiences of young women. The landscape has changed, in the sense that these harmful experiences now manifest both online and offline. While the online world has provided opportunity, knowledge and, at times, private support, in particular in the post COVID-19 era, virtual platforms have also provided a tool for 24/7 surveillance and abuse. Despite this new 'virtual' landscape, the experiences of street harassment in the form of 'catcalling', groping and sexual coercion continue to be an 'everyday occurrence'. Recollection of the normalisation of being judged by body shape during gym lessons, being groped on the bus or feeling pressured to have sex; essentially, the overwhelming gendered pressure and abuse continues.

While researching for this book, several people have asked me about my motivation and interest in this topic area. While the majority view this as an important issue to explore further, there are those commentators who continue to deny the presence of structural inequality, harmful gendered social norms and, indeed, abuse. In fact, I have had several 'discussions' focused on outlining the global evidence that clearly demonstrates the presence of gender-based violence (GBV). And yet there is this sense that, within a post-feminist society, equality has been achieved for women. At this point in the discussion, I always get a sense of two key issues: firstly, that there is a feeling that raising the issue is a nuisance, and, secondly, that there continues to be a wish by some men and women to remain ignorant of the extent of everyday harassment and abuse suffered, to a greater degree, by young women and women.

The aim of this book is to contribute original findings to the current academic debates on domestic abuse as a form of GBV. Firstly, an empirical contribution will be made to the growing literature on teenage intimate abuse in the UK via data gathered from a questionnaire and semi-structured interviews; secondly, the research findings further develop an under-researched area on gendered norms and abusive behaviour patterns within young intimate relationships by shifting the analytical focus to the social construction of the progression of these relationships; and, thirdly, the book offers findings in the aim of contributing to the debate on the development of prevention and early interventions to be used with young people in schools and beyond. The intention is to contribute to the academic debates by opening conversations with young women on their intimate relationships, by focusing on the progression of these relationships, the nature of abuse in them and young women's power within them.

Aligned to my identity and values as a social worker, the philosophical framework and lens underpinning this research was feminist theory and feminist research methods. The aim was to identify with participants as active agents, with a focus on their 'lived experiences'. The importance of re-focusing the power of agency for women and young women should not be underestimated, to ensure that there is space for effective action (Kelly, Sharp and Klein, 2014) by giving voice, choice and control to research participants. Mullender et al (2002) focused on the three Cs (consent, confidentiality and child protection) and the three Ds (distress, danger and disclosure) when planning and undertaking research with young people. Houghton (2015) expands on this framework with the addition of the three Es (enjoyment, empowerment and emancipation). This framework, as expanded upon by Houghton (2015), was considered throughout the planning and completion of this research, as the notion of giving young women positive empowerment central to the discussion throughout. Including children and young people in research focused on exploring sensitive topics allows us to better understand their experiences. As such, we need to give and transfer the power and the space so that young people become the storytellers and adults the listeners (Överlien, 2017).

I feel extremely lucky to be in the position to reflect upon and share the experiences of the young women of North Wales who contributed to this research project, and ultimately this book. Sharing time and space with these young women made me appreciate the opportunity I was provided to give them a 'voice' to share their attitudes and experiences. While the topic discussed was sensitive in nature, spending time in their space was often enjoyable, rewarding and educational! Working with two groups of young women as part of the research advisory group shaped my views on the project as a whole. My mantra for the group was that, despite the fact that I had experienced teenage intimate relationships, without a time machine or a ground-breaking face cream, my experiences were not within the current societal context. I worked with both groups for months, often staying to have lunch with the advisory group members. Not intending a cliché, I felt privileged to gain access to their world. Without a doubt, gaining their views on all aspects of the research tools was invaluable. I got some things horribly wrong, from including vodka rather than WKD as the alcohol of choice in a vignette, to translating the documents from English to Welsh in a manner that was judged by the young women as being too formal! They commented that my Welsh translation needed to include more 'slang' terms.

It also made me reflect on my Welsh identity, including our language, which has a gender-neutral term for boyfriend/girlfriend (cariad), which proved a challenge when carefully considering translation options.

I have written this book during the COVID-19 global pandemic. This has been a period of fear, change and the emergence of an as yet unknown future based on several perceived ideas of a 'new normal'. During this period, there have also been increased levels of abuse, including a new meaning of the idea of the 'hidden' nature of abuse during unprecedented periods of national lockdown. The hope is that the landscape for change is on the horizon, in particular as the Domestic Abuse Bill was granted royal assent and is now the Domestic Abuse Act (2021). Part of this change will focus on extending the offence of disclosing private sexual photographs and films with intent to cause distress to also cover threats to disclose intimate images.

The social policy changes and ongoing debates on related matters, such as the age of sexual consent, the non-consensual circulation of sexualised images, the exploitation of young women and the debates around the #MeToo movement focused on addressing sexual abuse and harassment, present the ideal context for this book. The murder of Sarah Everard in the UK in March 2021 has provided the platform for raising questions around the safety of women in public spaces, including the right to freedom from harassment, abuse and violence. This conversation has led to discussion around sexual agency and harassment across public spaces, including school settings. Following testimonials on the website Everyone's Invited, which is a social movement focused on eradicating rape culture, key changes will be implemented. The NSPCC–led Abuse in Education helpline was also established to offer support to survivors of sexual harassment, abuse and assaults in schools. During April and May 2021, it was reported that more than 350 calls were received by this helpline (NSPCC, 2021). The government launched an Ofsted review focusing on safeguarding measures to review procedures for addressing peer-on-peer abuse in schools and colleges. The terms of reference for the review concentrated on three key areas: safeguarding and curriculum, multi-agency safeguarding arrangements and victims' voice and reporting. This also included a review of the adequacy of school relationships and sex education and the personal, social, health and economic curriculum and teaching (Ofsted, 2021). Therefore, there are growing conversations on everyday harassment and abuse across media platforms, with the re-focus on the harmful impact of social and cultural norms. This re-focus, albeit ignited by horrific examples of violence and abuse, is intended to shift the power dynamics by challenging everyday abusive behaviour, which has been both minimised and accepted across society. Giving power to young women/women to share their experiences of a continuum of abusive behaviour is a progressive step in giving young women an equitable voice.

Understanding Abuse in Young People's Intimate Relationships is based on a feminist doctoral thesis, which had three key aims: to give voice to the attitudes and experiences of young women; to outline the key findings of the study; and to provide recommendations focused on a whole-community approach to address this social problem. My hope is that this book gives voice to young women by focusing on their everyday attitudes and experiences through exploring how they negotiate their identity and power within their intimate relationships. While a range of intersectional factors influencing the presence of violence and abuse within intimate relationships exists, the primary factor considered within this study was the construction of gender norms, abuse and power. This book aims to expand on current debates on the nature of young intimate relationships by exploring the progression of these relationships and young women's experiences of a continuum of abusive behaviour within them, with an exploration of their identity and how their limited choices are negotiated through their embodied practices within the relationships, thus contributing to our understanding of the everyday conceptualisations and experiences of young women. There is limited qualitative research with young women focusing on understanding the power dynamics, the influence of social norms and exploring the nature of abuse within young people's intimate relationships, an exception being recent qualitative research with young women in Sweden and Norway (Øverlien, Hellevik and Korkmaz, 2020).

There continues to be limited intersectional analysis of this social problem, in particular, our understanding of intersecting social positions. It must also be remembered that the concepts of 'dating', 'going out', 'seeing someone', being in an intimate relationship and a sense of courtship differ across cultures, lifestyles and places. We also need to consider the dynamics of both online and offline intimate relationships, in particular, when evaluating the similarities and differences between both forms of abuse. How we define intimate relationships, young people and, indeed, abuse can also differ across spaces and cultures. The definitions adopted should consider cultural dynamics and the context and nature of this form of abuse.

The key arguments in this book will explore the 'doing of gender' in social interactions situated within young intimate relationships, within schools and peer groups. The discussion will focus on the implications when young women perform a role contrary to the traditional gender role, resulting in abuse, coercion, control, bullying and being ostracised from their community and peer group. I reflect on and evaluate young women's attitudes and experiences of their intimate relationships and how these may conform to and challenge established gender norms and distinct sex categories. Chapter 1 introduces the research project with a particular focus on discussing how the voices of young women shaped the overall design and focus of the research. This chapter will concentrate on several key tensions and nuances around the meaning(s) of gender, which require further unpacking within the context of young intimate relationships, and therefore forms the basis of this book. It will also situate the study within the current research landscape and outline the key themes to be further investigated. The discussion ahead will further situate and expand upon the key themes of gendered attitudes, sexual double standards, the impact of social media and the nature and patterns of abuse in young intimate relationships. While these themes will be explored in more depth, this chapter will begin to emphasise some of the central tensions faced by young women within their relationships.

Chapter 2 moves the discussion forward with a detailed focus on exploring the nature and patterns of abuse within young intimate relationships. The focus is on highlighting the severity and impact of intimate partner abuse on young women, with a specific emphasis on exploring the continuum of abuse. This includes looking into the nature of coercive control and the psychological harm inflicted by such abuse, as well as everyday forms of harassment, such as sexual bullying, including groping, and gendered patterns of verbal abuse in schools and beyond. The discussion within this chapter will also begin to explore the impact of abusive behaviour on young women's well-being and identity.

The discussion in Chapter 3 will focus on exploring the impact of gendered social norms of relationship roles, in particular, the power dynamics during each stage of the progression of young intimate relationships. The sense of the gendered social construction of intimate relationships will be explored – basically, the norm or cultural feature of courtship – discussing the perceived benefits and comfort gained from accepting established gendered scripts, rather than suffering the consequences of non-conformity. Young men have social permission and expectations to focus on the physicality of intimate relationships, while young women experience the ingrained fear of transgressing gender norms and challenging this sexual emphasis, thus placing them within the quandary of 'sexual double standards'. Young women lack the power to operationalise their egalitarian attitudes in order to engage in relationships that adhere to the description of what they expect, want or desire within a 'healthy relationship'. As a default position, they rely and draw upon normative scripts which are focused on essentialist beliefs. The idea that young women undertake daily 'impression management' of performing both the 'doing of gender' and their perceived 'ideal girlfriend' role, often to their own detriment, will also be explored. Young women demonstrate how they carefully manage their 'performance of self' and the management of their own identity. It will be argued that barriers preventing the operationalisation of their attitudes, beliefs, wishes and feelings reinforce gender differences, providing unstable grounding for a change towards 'real' gender equality. The chapter will conclude by highlighting that young women perform what they see as the expected girlfriend role to satisfy the needs of their audience – essentially, to maintain what Goffman (1955) termed as 'facework' and paying 'lip service' to their boyfriends' demands, to the detriment of their own self-development of identity.

Chapter 4 will focus on the complexity of the deconstruction of female sexuality and the contradictory constructions of femininity that promote sexual allure while also asserting control over female sexuality. This dichotomy of a slag/angel and the gendered 'sexual double standards' is a key theme explored, and appears as a challenging dilemma for young women from their attitudinal understanding and experiences. The discussion will concentrate on the pressure on young women to perform the overt sexual role which is aligned to being a 'slag/slut'. Despite acknowledgement by young women that this is problematic and an unfair label, it is perpetuated by young women themselves. Pervasive 'double standards' exist in relation to girls' and boys' sexual activity, which function as a dichotomy for young women of angelic femininity and the stigmatised sexual slut/slag/whore, illustrating the precarious nature of their sexual reputation, in sharp contrast to young men's laddish/sexual hero role; thus, it is permitted and expected for young men to focus on the physicality of intimate relationships. The ingrained fear of transgressing gender norms and challenging this sexual emphasis places young women within the quandary of 'sexual double standards'. The discussion will explore how the 'doing' of sex for young women ignites a web of controversy and dilemma, often placing them in an impossible position.

The influence of social media or 'online' relationships has changed the nature of communication in relationships and is integral in shaping the landscape of young people's peer and intimate relationships. Chapter 5 explores how the nature of interpersonal communication has shifted, due to the widespread use of the internet and mobile phones, and so has the possibility for emotional abuse, specifically, the ability to remotely monitor movements. The dilemma of the internet, with its ability to perpetuate abuse by functioning as a platform to facilitate bullying behaviour, grooming and the non-consensual circulation of sensitive sexual images, but which can equally function as a supportive tool with vast information privately at young women's fingertips, will be a central discussion point of this chapter.

Chapter 6 will move to concentrate on the foundation of prevention education for young people. The focus is on promoting the need to develop a policy of 'healthy relationship' education that concentrates on a 'whole-community approach' that includes tackling gender norms as its foundation. The policy should go beyond the school setting in order to incorporate key multi-agency stakeholders, parents/carers and the wider community as a whole. The closing chapter will finalise the discussion by focusing on the argument that gender norms shape young women's power and space to operationalise their attitudes and beliefs of gender equality within their own intimate relationships. It will identify the impact of gendered expectations on young women's abilities to navigate the 'uncharted territory' of young intimate relationships. Young women continue to face challenges when negotiating their feminine identity. Prevention programmes geared towards empowering them should focus on promoting their confidence and individual agency. This re-evaluation will assist young women to construct their position in a manner that reduces the likelihood that any form of negotiation and power comes at a cost. This cost, seen within their narratives, was the emotion work of the management of this power imbalance and the requirement to 'subtly' perform their expected girlfriend role, due to the lack of negotiating space within their intimate relationships. The gaps between young women's attitudes, their desires, expectations and 'everyday' experiences, draw attention to the complex dilemma for young women when performing their role in intimate relationships.

While the conclusion reflects on the discussion and the future direction of policy and practice to address abuse in young intimate relationships, the landscape for change remains uncertain. The impetus for change appears to have the momentum of the new Domestic Abuse Act (2021) and the promise of an Ofsted review of peer-on-peer sexual harassment and abuse in schools. The commitment to sustain attitude and cultural changes that scaffold unhealthy gendered social norms remains uncertain. This should not deter us from our civic and moral duty of challenging abusive and harmful social norms and behaviour.

1

Framing young women's voices

All the views and experiences shared by the young women throughout this research project were invaluable. Having an insight into their everyday experiences reopened my eyes to many aspects of young women and women's intimate lives. When I say reopened my eyes, this space that was created between me and the young women who worked with me to both shape this project and participate in it made me revisit my own attitudes and experiences. There are key views shared during the discussion with the young women which have created a foundation for this book, including their views on equality, their emotion work, their lack of power or control, their lack of choices and the nature of the abuse experiences, including online bullying, sexual harassment and coercive sex. There was also the overwhelming notion of young men 'in a mood' and young women as 'slags and sluts'. Key quotes from the young women framed my ideas, while constantly making me reflect on my own identity.

The views shared by the young women will stay with me, and have indeed shaped my perspective on the harmful impact of gendered social norms, the way that young women wear a 'mask' to manage their identity to meet the requirements of social norms and the ultimate impact on their well-being. Aleysha's narrative illustrates key issues that will be explored throughout this book, specifically, the social norms that dictate the behaviour of both young women and young men. Aleysha's view also demonstrates the consequences for young women and the power of young men.

Interviewer:	So if the boy cheats, it's seen as quite a positive thing?
Aleysha:	Between the boys, they call each other a 'lad'.
Interviewer:	What happens to girls when they cheat?
Aleysha:	That's a massive thing, I think. Recently, there's been a massive thing going on, and she [the girl who cheated] got publicly humiliated, all on Facebook; it was horrible. It was the most horrible thing ever.
Interviewer:	Who did that to her?
Aleysha:	Her ex.
Interviewer:	What did he do?
Aleysha:	He put pictures up of her. Ones that she, like, trusted him with.
Interviewer:	Were they private pictures?

Aleysha:	Yeah. Just horrible.
Interviewer:	What did the pictures show?
Aleysha:	Her body.
Interviewer:	So they were, like, nudies.
Aleysha:	Yeah.
Interviewer:	Were there certain comments attached to them?
Aleysha:	It was just, like, cheating slag and ... it was horrible. He did take it down, but it's still there because everyone still seen and it's just ... if a boy had done that, most girls would have just gone home and cried, probably. I think boys have a streak in them, like ... to want to publicly humiliate girls if they do something to them.

Glain's advice "If you're subtle it's OK" around how to manage your identity and negotiate the demands of social norms will be revisited throughout the discussion.

The voices of the young women shaped the foundation for this work, outlining several key influences which I will describe to 'set the scene' regarding the nature of the problem and to define the context of how I developed my ideas. This process of 'scene setting' is crucial in outlining my stance, in particular, as the definition, meaning(s) and scope of gender and femininities and the resulting implications for the lived experiences of young women are often debated by academics and practitioners. This book focuses on the meaning(s) of human conduct, specifically, the constructive and emergent nature of interactions within young intimate relationships. The emphasis is on how young women continually modify and negotiate their behaviours as a result of their interactions and how their understanding(s) influences existing and new definitions of behaviour within these relationships. Within this work, it is the interpersonal level of social interactions which is of most interest, in particular, when gender roles and sexuality are embodied and performed on a social, virtual/social media and intimate platform.

The idea of 'active agency' is used to describe how young women draw on and modify social, cultural and sexual scripts within their own intimate relationships, which are located in broader meaning(s), norms and societal processes, including gendered dating norms. The 'active' role of individuals in shaping their meanings is focused on the use of language and communication to interpret them. As members communicate with one another by means of symbols, for example, language, gestures and social cues, their social interactions are based on the meaning(s) given to these symbols (both consciously and unconsciously). Different ways of seeing these symbols affect the outcomes of social interactions, for example, the meaning(s) attributed to the label 'boyfriend/girlfriend', which in turn influences the nature of social interactions. The process of 'naming' within intimate relationships and peer groups can be based on power, for example, the use of negative labels/language attached to and associated with young women (sluts/slags/whores). The impact of the meaning(s) allocated to these labels subsequently shapes intimate and peer relationships. For young women, particular labels, which attach either negative or positive symbols, can shape the nature and meaning(s) of their social interactions, which are often negotiated within an unequal space – the 'typifying' of young women, for example, the expected role they should perform in the dating scene, on social media and within their intimate relationships. What you 'become' through social interaction is constantly negotiated in the aim of either maintaining positive symbols or changing negative symbols, which can then influence the actions undertaken. Not all social actors are conscious or 'active' actors, specifically, due to structural constraints on their power and choice. Individuals can often face limitations to their power when sharing their views, relating themselves to others or shaping their own identities. All large-scale structures are inevitably grounded in the symbolic constructs that individuals adopt, and therefore there is an automatic interest in the impact of power when analysing individual realities (Fine, 1993). Indeed, power cannot be assumed to be equal within everyday social interactions, and it is the intention of this book to empower young women to promote their active agency and their intersectional identities.

The idea of intersectionality was developed by Crenshaw (1989), focusing on the influence of intersecting attributes and positions, such as gender and race, and how these cross over to influence multiple oppressions and disadvantages. Therefore, this perspective rejects the idea of the woman or female standpoint, and conceptualises gender as being shaped through locations of structural and representational identities. As a result, the focus is on social relations and structural inequalities, due to the imbalance of power in society that shapes our identities. While understanding this intersectional perspective helps us to unpack the nuanced nature of young women's individual needs and identities, it must also be noted that the current framework in the UK of the Equality Act 2010 (which outlines the statutory protected characteristics) is yet to bring into force S14, which outlines combined discrimination based on dual characteristics (within a limited scope of only two characteristics). Due to this, claims of interlocking oppression on the basis of intersectional discrimination are limited beyond the scope of case law. I argue that social interaction is a process regulated by gendered social norms, specifically, young women's ability to maintain an equal role within their intimate relationships, as gender is socially constructed based on the inequality of power and control of those with more power (young men/men) over those with less power (young women/women).

'Doing gender' and the influence of social norms

The influence of harmful gendered norms on the prevalence of GBV on a global perspective is well known. Social norms have been defined as 'the informal, mostly unwritten, rules that define acceptable, appropriate, and obligatory actions in a given group or society' (Cislaghi and Heise, 2018, p 2). Generally, people in society follow the rules established through social norms, due to social pressures to comply, through the symbolism of reward of compliance and to normalise their behaviour or actions. Social norms can be both protective and harmful (Cislaghi and Heise, 2018) and intersect with factors such as power, control, structural inequalities and social relations. The definition of gender norms outlines the impact on agency and power:

> Gender norms are social norms that specifically define what is expected of a woman and a man in a given group or society. They shape acceptable, appropriate and obligatory actions for women and men (in that group or society), to the point that they become a profound part of people's sense of self. They are both embedded in institutions and nested in people's minds. They play a role in shaping women's and men's (often unequal) access to resources and freedoms, thus affecting women's and men's voice, agency and power. (Cislaghi, Manji and Heise, 2018, p 5)

Power is quintessential in the social construction of gender, as structural inequalities favouring men result in a lack of equality for women. Biological arguments of gendered division essentially result in the discrimination of women based on their biology and the oppressive biology of men, whereas, in contrast, social construction arguments focus on roles, stereotypes and essentially the subordination of women linked to expected and perceived gendered social norms. The degree of 'choice' around gender identity is restricted by our body, material circumstances and social position. Roles are gendered according to social experiences, beliefs and, to a lesser extent, individual opinion. The essence or the gendered identity of women is not purely dependent on gendered social norms. We construct our own identities based on cultural and social factors, influenced by life experiences and choice. This level and degree of choice is influenced not only by opportunities but also by social norms which favour male-gendered roles. The concept of social construction argues that power is external; power can play a key role in the construction of gendered identities. The social construction of gender suggests that gender roles are continually shaped and constructed. Conversely, societal hierarchy and the presumed reality of 'equality of compromise' are not commenced on equal power platforms, which is further compounded by societal feminine power division to challenge expected social gendered norms which impact on the fluidity of gendered identity roles.

It is acknowledged in academic literature that bodies develop gendered identities due to the constant 'doing' of attributes associated with masculinity or femininity (West and Zimmerman, 1987), which is an active social construct that can be 'undone' in particular circumstances (Deutsch, 2007). When considering the definition of gender, the concepts of the social construction of gender and power are prominent. The perspective that gender is a 'doing' rather than a 'being' is continuously embedded in everyday social interactions (West and Zimmerman, 1987). West and Zimmerman (1987, p 127) define gender as 'the activity of managing situated conduct in light of normative conceptions of attitudes and activities appropriate to one's sex category'. Anecdotally, the 'common-sense' view of gender is based on biological determinism, reinforced by the media perception of gender determined by DNA, hormones and sexual organs, with the symbolism of the phallus, vagina and breasts, constructing an outwardly physical image of gender. The essentialist view of gender is rejected here as relying on simplistic, dualistic categories of gender, in favour of the notion of gender as a fluid social construct evolving with societal changes, social interactions and individualised identities. Gender construction is primarily social, not biological, ultimately formed via socialised roles, responsibilities and normative behaviours. Gender is embedded across society in all aspects of daily living, be it within the family, work/labour, clothing, mannerisms or sex. The gender status of women affects the social construction of sexuality, fertility, pregnancy, childbirth and parenting, not the other way around. The gender labelling of children begins with parental social cues within the ambit of socially acceptable behaviour norms in order to encourage the 'doing of gender' in a particular manner (West and Zimmerman, 2002). For the purpose of this discussion, gender is defined as a social construct which enforces binary static roles and responsibilities for young men/men and young women/ women by dictating culturally ascribed and acceptable 'natural' behaviour which maintains social arrangements.

The impact of the social construction of gender is evident throughout society and is therefore the foundation for our gendered identities. Structural powers dictate gendered norms and inequalities associated with the concept of young men/men as active and controlling, and young women as passive and vulnerable (Connell, 1987). There is often a false common belief that young women are empowered, autonomous individuals, which is in contrast to the perceived normative feminine characteristics of passivity and respectability. The everyday challenges faced by young women are further compounded by the false belief that they have the same degree of power as their male counterparts.

Gender permeates all aspects of social life and sexuality is no exception. Gender and sexuality intersect, although sexuality cannot be directly moulded on to gender. Gender is constructed so that characteristics of femininity are undesirable and subordinate to those of masculinity; this in turn limits the role and sexuality of young women within their intimate relationships (Tolman et al, 2016). As part of everyday life, we 'do' gender in two ways: firstly, as a practical accomplishment of interpretive interaction, and, secondly, through practical activities, for example, having sex (Jackson and Scott, 2010, p 92). The intersection of gender and sexuality are continuous and observable, which can be problematic. The definition of sexuality is subjective; what is sexual to one person may not be to another.

Despite the belief that the presence of a sexual double standard favouring men over women has been eroded with time, the dominance of male sexual pleasure remains, which in turn limits female sexual desire. Women have less status, power and control within their intimate relationships, as they are subjected to a 'double standard' that supports and promotes men, limiting their autonomy and sexuality and resulting in oppression. This gendered 'double standard' impacts on a wider spectrum of behaviour, including their agency of appearance, social activities, employment and leisure activities. The sexuality of young women has primarily been linked to biological essentialist views, focused on the misconception of young women as lacking desire (Fine, 1988) and therefore passive to the sexual demands of young men/ men. This perceived 'natural' role of women as lacking sexual desire while preferring love is in opposition to the construction of what is 'natural' for men, specifically, the stereotype of 'hyper-sexuality'. Social norms dictate that women are required to be passive until their desires are activated by men (Jackson and Scott, 2010). It is therefore expected that young men/ men take the lead and initiate sexual intimacy.

As discussed, sexuality is a social construct established by prescribed 'sexual scripts' informed by our social interactions, which are focused on 'learning' sexual behaviour, including our wants and desires (Gagnon and Simon, 1973). Young people also assimilate their environment, including being influenced and socialised by social media and their peers. Essentially, our continued understanding of sexuality and the sexual scripts we draw upon are shaped by the perceived 'natural' gendered power and control favouring men.

Goffman's presentation of self

Goffman (1959) maintained that social interactions, or the 'doing' of gender, should be studied as an enactment in a theatrical performance (the dramaturgical model). Social life was conceptualised as a staged drama, with the idea of 'the self' and social ritual core principles, linked to our sense of self, the notion of our inner and outer self and identity. Similar to actors on a stage, we use strategies of impression management, providing information and cues to others that present us in the most favourable light (Goffman, 1959, 1963, 1971). In their capacity as performers, individuals are concerned with maintaining the impression that they are 'living up' to particular normative standards, therefore 'staging' the identity of particular gendered roles. Goffman saw individuals as 'social actors', depending on props as if everyday communication was a staged performance, with dialect and costumes used as dramatic devices to produce a shared sense of reality. The focus is on the presentation of self and the division between the outer and inner self, the playwright, producer, actor and part. The adoption of theatrical metaphors of 'performances', the front-stage performance and the back-stage 'self' performance, is used to explore the nature of human interaction. The focus is on the 'front-' and 'back-stage' areas, including the tensions between both roles, with the 'back' concentrated on the preparation of the performance and the illusion of one's self-presentation, with gossip regarded as 'staging talk'. This idea of the influence of 'back-' and 'front-stage' presentation of self will be discussed further with reference to the analysis of young people's behaviours within their intimate relationships, specifically their 'personal front(s)'. As part of this self-presentation, various symbols are employed, for example, cues, hints and expressive gestures, emphasising the reliance on appearance, the 'mask of performance' and the requirement for the capacity to switch enacted roles. As such, we are embodied social actors. As if communication was a staged drama, the flow of information across daily conversations is often controlled by social norms, but is also concealed as if it were a drama to ensure the control of our individual situated self. To perform is to be an active actor that plays a role to control the flow of information and manage situations, for example, shameful situations. Social actors manipulate the presentation of 'self' to present a favourable performance (Goffman, 1959).

As seen in later chapters, social stigma also plays a key part in the performance of everyday social interactions. We maintain 'face' by following social norms to present the 'ideal' image of ourselves, essentially using 'facework' to maintain the ritual order of social interaction (Goffman, 1967). Failing to adhere to social rituals or invading another's self is contrary to social norms (Goffman, 1983). The idea of 'aggressive facework' involves selecting a victim for whom the audience will have little sympathy (Goffman, 1959). Goffman (1963) identified how individuals defined as being subject to 'aggressive facework' and therefore having 'spoiled identities' will face challenges when negotiating their social environment. This is due to the lack of acceptance of them by others, as people's reactions can 'spoil' or negatively influence individual identities. As a form of protection or self-preservation, 'protective face measures' are adopted to 'save face' and function as a protective buffer (Goffman, 1967). These measures include politeness, employing discretion, ambiguity or withdrawing from an interaction or conversation.

Goffman (1967) also examined how the gap between the macro and micro social worlds could be bridged. He believed that we consider ourselves and others when we act, which he conceptualised as 'ritual'. Goffman (1974) acknowledged the impact of structures on communication and interactions, specifically, how interactions are 'framed', with the existence of formal and informal rules to prevent 'outsiders' from joining, therefore connecting the interaction order to the production and reproduction of social structures, illustrating the relations of power in social life. He saw 'self-identity' as a social product dependent on the validation of performances aligned to social norms, with individual ability to sustain self-image for others dependent on access to structural resources and the possession of desirable attributes.

The exploration of Goffman's model, and what Lamont (2014) terms as 'symbolic gendering', will influence the shape of the discussion ahead, in particular, the gendered norms, cultural practices and the young women's navigation of negotiating relationship scripts associated with dating traditions and relationship progression. Abusive behaviour within intimate relationships is gendered, primarily due to the structural gendered power dynamics within society which favour young men/men. It is argued that the social construction of masculinity and the presence of structural inequalities which perpetuate gendered norms dictate normative scripts for both genders. These gendered norms provide the foundation for young people's attitudes and expectations of their role and identity – gender as a social construct, if further shaped as a result of power, oppression and GBV. The 'relationship' scripts of young women are governed by feminine heterosexuality linked to gender norms, inequality and the status of the hegemonic male, which highlights the binary of defining women relational to the power held by men. Young women's voices can offer an alternative 'script' to challenge social norms and stereotypes in a society manifested by men.

The research study

This book is about listening to and hearing the voices of young women, with a focus on empowering young women to share their attitudes and experiences. As I endeavoured to spend time with the young women who were central to the research project, they became much more than research participants. By spending time with them, my understanding of their everyday education environment, their likes, dislikes, how they dressed and how they formed friendships assisted me in establishing their everyday perspectives on their intimate relationships. My observations and later my understanding of their attitudes, experiences and social cues have informed the discussion in this book. The intention was to allow and enable young women to articulate and discuss their attitudes towards, and experiences of, intimate relationships.

The book outlines the findings of a mixed-methods study, exploring how gender norms influence the nature and patterns of behaviour within young intimate relationships, including how their interactions shape their individual identities, their power to progress these relationships and also the nature and patterns of abuse as part of the relationships. The focus was on understanding how young women (aged 15–18 years old) define and conceptualise particular behaviours within their own intimate relationships, and how this subsequently impacts on their identity and well-being. Each stage of this research endeavoured to give voice to the young women to promote them as active research participants. The empirical work for this study involved the completion of a questionnaire (n=220) and semi-structured interviews (n=25) with young women aged 15–18, conducted in seven schools and the youth justice services in North Wales. Specifically, the research process was separated into three key stages:

1. Advisory stage: Two advisory groups were established in order to co-produce the research documents and research tools. This space allowed the young women to provide feedback on the questions, language use and the use of particular interview techniques, for example, vignettes. Research demonstrates the benefits of including young people in research projects, not only to provide them with a 'voice' (Article 12 UNCRC) but also to assist them in developing transferable skills (Kirby, 2004; Shaw et al, 2011) and provide them with audience and influence (Lundy, 2007).
2. Questionnaire stage: The fieldwork commenced with an attitude questionnaire (n=220) on young women's attitudes towards GBV, including their perspectives on broader gender norms, gender norms within relationships, the use of social media (such as sexting, Snapchatting and Facebook) and a spectrum of abuse in intimate relationships. The questionnaire assisted in establishing 'lines of inquiry' and in isolating key themes to be explored within the qualitative interviews.
3. Interview stage: Interviews were completed in order to gather a sense of the participants' 'lived experiences', to triangulate the questionnaire data and to capture a more nuanced understanding of their perceptions of their intimate relationships. Within the sample school sites, 25 young women participated in the qualitative stage. Semi-structured interviews were used in order to allow some flexibility and provide participants with a degree of 'power'. Vignettes were used as part of both stages in order to assist with 'setting the scene' in a non-threatening manner (Shaw et al, 2011; Elliffe, Holt and Øverlien, 2020).

The feminist nature of this research: empowering young women as 'active agents'

A 'golden thread' throughout this book is the feminist nature of the research, which is embodied in the topic and the research design. There is a general belief that gender equality has been achieved. In reality, the gap between the perception of equality and the actual degree of it continues (McRobbie, 2007). Young women in particular struggle with their perceived understandings and attitudes focused on a contemporary fantasy of equality and equity. The key tenet of feminism is the political perspective to strive for change in order to challenge the oppression of women. Feminist theories span a spectrum of beliefs and perspectives across feminist movements and ideologies. Feminism is generally driven by the rejection of essentialism, due to the belief of gender as a social construct. Within this understanding is the idea that the myriad of sexist oppressions is due to the biological and social construction of being a woman, equating to everyday sexism and abuse because of the unequal dynamics, as men possess more economic, cultural and social resources than women. Historically, feminist researchers have faced increased pressure to justify the validity of their knowledge, methods and subjectivity in light of perceived political bias. Despite criticism, the general nature of feminist research is focused on exploring social power, scientific oppression and promoting social and political activism (Miner et al, 2012).

The feminist methodology adopted for this research was the notion of conceptualising young women as 'active agents', framing the incorporation of the 'voices' of young women into research about and for them. This conceptualisation promotes the inclusion of children and young people in research looking at their everyday lived experiences. Young people are theorised as autonomous or 'active agents' capable of constructing their relationship networks as social actors who are worthy of study in their own right. The active agency of young women was positively empowered, not only to inform the design of the research through the co-production of the research tools as part of the advisory groups but also to gather their attitudes towards gender norms and their experiences of intimate relationships within a space created for young women. The level of 'openness' of this research is in keeping with feminist methodology of allowing people to explain their wider meaning(s) as part of the process of giving young women a voice as research participants exploring a sensitive topic.

Positive empowerment of the participation of young women as 'active agents' is essential within an adult-centric society, as listening to their voices is important to empower them to develop their own agency. Aligned with feminist methodology, working closely with the advisory groups assisted in balancing the 'power' dynamics and facilitating continual inclusive reflection on the research activities. Feminist research demonstrates the strength of adapting research tools suited to the research participants to ensure clear comprehension, effective information retrieval and reporting. Essentially, focusing on reflective practice resulted in a more sensitive methodology (Borland, 1991). The two young women advisory groups formulated for this research assisted in balancing the power gap between the 'researcher and researched' by ensuring that the right questions were asked in the right manner.

Young voices: shaping the research tools

As part of the research 'performance', reflexivity has been fundamental to my positioning and my renegotiated sense of self. I strove to include myself in the young women's discussion of youth sub-cultural norms around clothing, accessories, music and TV shows. I found myself much more aware of my dress sense and, in particular, my handbag choice/ style (or lack of)! It appeared that the traditional school rucksacks had morphed into glamorous handbags, with particular designs and labels. The carrier bag and box carrying the stationary for the advisory sessions were quickly ditched in favour of a bag in keeping with their sense of style. I have never striven to 'fit in' with particular norms or styles, so this was a new experience for me. They also discussed particular activities they enjoyed in their leisure time. One activity described was watching the MTV show *Catfish*, an American reality series. The series focuses on the idea of online 'love'/relationships, with a person often 'duped' by someone establishing a false online persona. This particular role of social media was a concept germane to this research, around the impact of social media on relationships and its ability to perpetuate lies, humiliation and coercive control, both online and offline. Therefore, I quickly clicked on the series link of *Catfish* (much to my amazement, there is a film and four series), to get a sense of what it meant to be 'catfished'. Watching this series allowed me to identify with their interests, while also providing a reference point for discussing some of the issues around social media pertinent to the development of the research tools. I was genuinely interested in the young women, which assisted in establishing an authentic positionality in order to avoid the 'automatic aroma of fraud' (Patai, 1991, p 149). As our individual identities, life histories and differences weave a complex web beyond the notion of this potential superficial announcement of identity, re-evaluating my positionality was necessary in order to establish rapport and genuinely strive to understand their sub-cultures. The crucial skill was to avoid shifting my position and crossing the line into territory of adult patronisation or, worse still, exploitation. I genuinely enjoyed these interactions with the young women, with my own reflexivity a key element of my feminist praxis. Incorporating and diffusing young voices as experts in their own lives to shape the research tools proved invaluable to the research design.

The draft questionnaire contained three vignettes, included to stimulate discussion, as participants were invited to respond to hypothetical scenarios to elicit their views, beliefs and attitudes. The aim was to provide young women with the opportunity to position their views by responding to questions in another person's voice, with the vignettes addressing a sensitive topic in a non-threatening manner (Neale, 1999; Renold and Barter, 2000). The function of vignettes is to allow situational context to be explored and to clarify individual judgements on 'moral dilemmas' within the framework of a 'story' (Renold and Barter, 2000) to generalise, rather than personalise, situations. Vignettes also provided the opportunity for participants to have greater control over the interaction by enabling them to determine at what stage, if at all, they introduced their own experiences to illuminate their abstract responses. The scenarios were aligned with the research topic in an age-appropriate format, illustrating characters and scenarios from different perspectives – a victim, perpetrator and bystander – to elicit reflection and critical thinking. The vignettes were designed to be understandable, internally consistent, age-appropriate and aligned to the Welsh culture; for example, the characters mainly had Welsh names. However, despite this alignment with Welshness, other intersecting needs were incorporated as part of the research tools, for example, sexuality and age. A crucial aspect of the vignettes' design was receiving guidance and constructive feedback from the advisory group, primarily by asking its members to describe their immediate reaction to the stories, language and characters depicted. Again, a cognitive approach was adopted by asking the young women to share their views 'aloud' to stimulate constructive discussion and inform any amendments to the vignette. The comments reflected that a longer vignette with more details was preferred. One of the vignettes described that the couple were taking a bus home after a night out. However, the vignette was amended so that the boyfriend was characterised as older and had his own car. To some degree, this may appear to be a minor amendment; however, the discussion stimulated the allure of older boyfriends and some of the challenges they bring. Therefore, the impact of having an older boyfriend was identified as a key theme requiring greater emphasis in the questionnaire.

The 'check and balance' of gaining advice from a group of young women similar to the research sample group was particularly useful when they questioned the following aspects of the draft vignette: "I don't think vodka is the type of alcoholic beverage I would drink – maybe WKD or lager. But, to be honest, vodka is drank, but on its own" (comment on vignette 1). This discussion was most certainly one of the most memorable moments for me. In the draft version of vignette 1, during the party, the young people were originally drinking vodka. I was strongly advised that this was not their alcoholic beverage of choice, which rendered a less authentic vignette. I promptly changed this aspect of the vignette and poked fun at myself, primarily that I needed a time machine or better face cream to take me back to my youth! Positioning myself as genuinely requiring their guidance but also acting on their advice empowered their position and assisted in gaining their trust. I endeavoured to position myself as separate from the school staff, including framing my role as a postgraduate student from the university and acknowledging my comfort with being addressed by my first name rather than the formal labelling of the 'Miss' or 'Sir' of their school. Not only was this crucial in a practical sense in order to ensure the clarity of my identity and role, but also to ensure that the young women felt comfortable to discuss issues about their teachers, for example, their likelihood of seeking advice and guidance from them.

I also distanced myself from my professional background as a social care and criminal justice manager, which appeared to strengthen my focus on my role as a researcher and my commitment to 'partnership' in striving to recognise and address power imbalances. Despite my willingness to discuss my identity and history, I opted not to openly discuss my previous role working both in social services and youth justice, to avoid confusion around 'which professional hat I was wearing' and also any pre-conceived ideas of my previous professional experience. However, my previous work experience and commitment to social work values of empowerment and anti-oppressive practice assisted with my reflections.[1] Also, as an ex-professional from the area, I saw myself as an 'insider'. Without doubt, my local knowledge, awareness of the local Welsh nuances and ability to speak Welsh assisted in reinforcing my 'insider' position. Despite these commonalities between the students and me, there were several key differences. Despite my efforts to understand the young women's language, culture and emotional cues, age was an obvious key difference. On reflection, as part of the group discussion, my lack of knowledge of 'their' generation was a key discussion point I used to gain their insight and attitudes towards relevant topics to my research, for example, sexting. Despite the reinforcement of the age and power gap, the young advisors revelled in their position of advising and educating me on their sub-cultures and daily norms. This was evidenced on several occasions, for example: "Shall I mark my views on the sheet for you?" and "We need an adult away from the school to come and talk to us about these things, like you from the university".

Being listened to and asked about their thoughts appeared to empower young women to share their views with me in a similar manner to voicing their thoughts with their peers. Consequently, despite my acknowledgement of the age difference to stimulate their role as advisors, their response was to communicate with me as if I was their peer. While I positioned myself differently to the students, they highlighted our similarities and my difference to their teachers, as I was from the university and treated them as young adults. I also endeavoured to continuously build rapport by spending time at the school and being visibly present, for example, having lunch in the school canteen with the young women. Therefore the 'insider' and 'outsider' roles were fluid and interchangeable, with both positions illustrating benefits in shifting the landscape of the 'researcher and researched' power dynamics.

With regard to the statement on Marc's financial control of Nia's money in vignette 1 ("It's so kind of Marc to keep Nia's money and to pay for everything"), the advisory groups wanted further information to explicitly reflect this point. A few comments were received that the final statement, "he just doesn't see the point of 'carrying on' without her", was not explicit enough to distinguish whether he was making threats to hurt/kill himself or finish his relationship with Nia. However, the researcher left this point unchanged and explained that this was to allow more 'open' feedback and trigger discussion during the qualitative stage of the research. Therefore, the majority of their suggestions were adopted within the questionnaire to be piloted, with the young women growing in confidence as their suggestions were accepted and incorporated within the amended version.

There needed to be a balance of encouraging freedom of expression and language use within an advisory group setting but also being ready to challenge any use of offensive language within a learning environment. This was not identified as an issue; however, on the other side of this spectrum, the young women within Group 1 appeared eager to please and provide responses that were perceived to be socially desirable. As the advisory group sessions progressed, the young women settled into a 'comfort zone' as discussions were more challenging, comfortable and reflective. While this 'comfortable' group dynamic felt more natural, some participants began to discuss their views openly.

The emergence of awareness around abuse in teenage relationships and sexualisation was generally illustrated within the advisory discussions, as members were aware of previous campaigns (This is Abuse) and popular discussion of this issue (*Hollyoaks*). Despite a mature approach to this topic, their awareness was limited to particular behaviour on the continuum of abuse, primarily rape and physical harm rather than coercion and harassment. However, members did not voice attitudes or beliefs that reinforced victim blame as previously identified (McCarry, 2012), potentially demonstrating the impact of this emerging awareness. This study confirmed that involving young people in sensitive research should not always be topic-led. The advisory process worked as a filter to deliver robust methods, but also encouraged a shift in power dynamics in favour of inclusion. Witnessing the outcome of their work, and moving away from tokenistic participation, fuelled the young women's willingness to contribute. Indeed, as the sessions progressed, they became more enthused in their involvement in the advisory groups, moving towards increased participation. However, mutual benefits can only be reaped if the ethical planning, in particular around working in partnership with gatekeepers, is maintained. Quantifying the mutual benefits of a facilitated advisory group is challenging, not only due to a pre-conceived notion of benefits but also because of the need to evaluate the 'real' mutual benefits. As a general evaluation of the advisory group process, a 'head, heart, carrier bag and dustbin' form was circulated, focusing on what the young women had learnt, what they had felt, what they would take away and anything that they would leave behind. Participants reported feeling valued and listened to, being treated with respect and encouraged to be confident and voice their views. Interestingly, the only 'item' they would 'bin' were the views shared in the groups and any personal aspect of our discussions. This brought our discussion on ground rules and confidentiality 'full circle', as the idea of privacy and confidentiality was a theme embedded in each stage of the evaluation responses, that is, in what they felt was important, respectful, a learning point and a 'keepsake'.

Reflections

The advisory sessions provided the opportunity to observe the context and environment for locating young women's attitudes and norms in their daily culture. Gaining an overall impression of how young women communicate and the common language used not only assisted with the research design but also in building rapport and knowledge to prepare for the fieldwork stages of the research. Generally, the findings from the advisory groups and pilot sessions demonstrate the richness (complex and occasionally contradictory) of young women's perspectives. Excluding young women from participating in research on GBV due to concerns of causing distress is paternalistic and fails to provide this cohort with the opportunity to express their views. It also limits the opportunity to learn from their experiences. Moving away from a paternalistic, protectionist approach is a key benefit voiced by these advisory groups. Excluding children and young people from research on the basis of protecting 'their best interests' further perpetuates the marginalisation of their views. Although GBV is regarded as a sensitive topic, working effectively with gatekeepers, conducting relevant risk assessments and thorough preparation provide the necessary safeguards. Ethically, young women should have the opportunity to advise and participate in 'too adult-centric' research topics, rather than being sheltered from discussing 'sensitive issues', which does not offer actual protection from distress. In broader terms, research with young people should be focused on ethical practice grounded in positive empowerment, respect, promotion of well-being and the establishment of a common dialogue between young participants and the researcher. The ultimate aim here, as suggested by other research (see Elliffe, Holt and Øverlien, 2020), is to make young women visible in research, practice and policy developments.

2

The nature and patterns of abuse in young intimate relationships

The change in the Home Office (non-statutory) definition of domestic violence and abuse in March 2013 to include 16–17 year olds began to shift the attention towards young people, and towards a pattern of abusive behaviour. The key focus of the changes implemented was to include young people as potential survivors of domestic violence and abuse, and to include coercive control as part of the definition in order to assist us to acknowledge the trends in abusive behaviour patterns. Shifting the emphasis on to coercive behaviour concentrates on a pattern of behaviour, power and control, rather than maintaining a focus on a singular incident, which aims to foster a progressive understanding of GBV.

The Serious Crime Act 2015 (Section 76) outlined a new offence of controlling or coercive behaviour, demonstrated as part of an intimate or familial relationship, which carries a maximum sentence of five years' imprisonment, a fine or both. The new offence closed a gap in the law around patterns of controlling or coercive behaviour in an ongoing relationship between intimate partners or family members. The adoption of the Istanbul Convention (2011) and the publication of the landmark UK Domestic Abuse Act (2021) also signals developments in the right direction, with the responsibilities of all member states who have ratified the Istanbul Convention to adhere to the four key pillars of prevention, protection, prosecution and coordinated policies. While the UK may comply with key aspects of the Istanbul Convention, the Convention remains unratified in the country. As a result, there is no legal requirement to comply with the minimum standards, with no firm date to ratify this international agreement on the horizon in the UK. This omission can be linked to the significant delay in implementing the Domestic Abuse Bill, which was years in the making.

The discussion within this chapter will begin to explore key differences in the nature, patterns and visibility of abuse in young intimate relationships, in comparison with adult intimate relationships.

Naming and defining the issue

On a global perspective, women are regarded as the group most at risk of suffering abuse (Watts and Zimmerman, 2002). Defining, conceptualising and deconstructing the abuse and violence suffered by women within their intimate relationships has historically been complex. The violence and abuse of women can take several forms and be understood subjectively, with different signs, symptoms and behaviour acknowledged or ignored as abusive. A myriad of factors contribute to this challenge, including gendered attitudes, beliefs and a lack of acceptance of particular behaviour as 'everyday sexism' (Bates, 2014). The lack of understanding of the gendered symmetry of violence/abuse (Kimmel, 2002), and the influence of wider structural power inequalities, further confuse the issue.

GBV is a social problem embedded across societies, rooted in the inequity of power based on gender, supported by structural inequalities and institutional power in the form of control, laws and policies dictated by hegemonic gendered social norms. Gendered roles function as a primary social system for distributing power to ensure that this power is utilised 'every day' through our gender. Polar gendered roles based on unequal power result in the utilisation of violence and abuse in order to maintain dominance, not only to rule but also to sabotage the change of this pattern. Violence and abuse are synonymous with 'supremacy' and 'masculinity', whereas 'weak' or 'sensitive' men are described as 'feminine'. GBV is not simply violence but a form of power, control and degradation of women's bodies, minds and souls via hegemonic masculinity. Male 'successes' often involve influence over the lives of others, with failure ridiculed. Of course, not all men are violent or abusive, but the power men acquire throughout societal settings as a result of their gender is evident in their status. The general lack of opposition to the concept of masculinity results in the automatic power accorded to men, irrespective of their personal attributes or skills, and is a given based on gender. This power and control accorded to men ensures that the violence towards, and abuse of, women is both supported and perpetuated as an accepted social norm. The socially expected ideas and values related to gender shape how men view themselves as men, in particular, regarding their expected power within their intimate relationships. Although differences between men and women are much less notable in more progressive or equitable societies, all societies tend to confer a higher social value on men than on women, and a range of norms and powers derive from this.

The meaning(s) of abuse within intimate relationships should be fluid, 'everyday' and normalised. Focusing on a continuum of abusive behaviours allows for this 'everyday' understanding of GBV. A continuum is not focused on constructing the seriousness on a linear line linking experiences, or a hierarchy of abuse, but is based on a myriad of forms of sexism and oppression experienced daily by women. Therefore, abuse is illustrated as the norm, rather than sporadic or abnormal occurrences, recognising the overlapping of different behaviours and the commonality of the experiences of these behaviours. This concept of a gendered continuum of abuse links women's experiences with the common causes and consequences of abuse which are informed by gendered inequality, social norms, roles and expectations of masculinity and femininity. The notion of a continuum is essential in connecting and contextualising young women's everyday experiences of their intimate relationships to harmful gendered social norms.

Review of the evidence

There is elevated normalisation of abuse and controlling behaviour among young people (CAADA, 2013). Evidence suggests significant trends of peer violence and abuse across younger relationships, illustrating this behaviour as the norm rather than the exception in the UK (Barter et al, 2009; Wood et al, 2011; Berelowitz et al, 2012; Fox et al, 2013) and globally (Chung, 2005; Barter et al, 2015). The degree of harm is clearly evidenced, as is the gendered nature of this harm (Barter et al, 2009; Berelowitz et al, 2012; Sundaram, 2014). While there is an emerging comprehensive body of research covering diverse aspects of the dynamics of such relationships, particular categories of young people, such as pregnant young women, young mothers, young women in secure settings and disabled young women, are yet to receive detailed research attention.

Research on teenage GBV and abuse has been undertaken in Canada, Australia and, more prominently, in the US, where a substantial body of research exists focusing on 'dating violence'. UK-based studies have focused on the prevalence and patterns of abuse within young intimate relationships, in comparison with the research conducted in the US, which has concentrated on dating violence, primarily targeting college and university students. While it has been of benefit to draw upon these studies, there are significant differences between the UK and the US, in particular, around 'dating' norms. The majority of US-based research on this topic has primarily focused on large-scale surveys and the prevalence of physical and sexual violence measured against adult-centric tools (for example, the conflict tactic scale), which cannot be easily applied to a UK context. It is also questionable whether US-based research can be generalised to the European culture and context (Hellevik, 2017). US evidence suggests that adolescent 'dating violence' emerges between the ages of 15 and 16, with these dating relationships mirroring patterns identified in college and adult relationships, primarily, the abuse of power and the inability of survivors to leave abusive relationships (Makepeace, 1981; Wolfe et al, 1997). Furthermore, substantial US evidence indicates a high prevalence of sexual and gendered violence in student communities (Fisher and Sloan, 2011), findings that studies in the UK echo (Barter et al, 2009; Wood et al, 2011; Fox et al, 2013). While the US has a rich body of research, there are less studies on the continuum of GBV. Therefore, the range of potential harms caused by a continuum of abuse is under-researched, both in the US and in the UK. This includes exploring the nature of coercive control and the psychological harm inflicted by such abuse, as well as everyday forms of harassment, such as sexual bullying, including groping, and gendered patterns of verbal abuse (for exceptions, see Ringrose, 2012; Fox et al, 2013; Zero Tolerance, 2014; McGlynn et al, 2017) in schools and beyond.

The following terms are used throughout, and are therefore defined from the outset. Young people's intimate relationships are defined as extra-familial intimate relationships, which include an element of dating and intimacy. The terms 'young people', 'young men', 'young women' and 'young person' will be adopted, with the exception of when other research specifies and makes reference to terms such as 'teenager', 'adolescent' and 'child'. While frequent reference is made to violence and abuse within relationships, the term 'abuse' will mostly be used as it recognises a continuum of harmful attitudes and behaviours within young people's intimate relationships. Reference will also be made to 'dating violence' when discussing US-based research.

Patterns in prevalence data

Research across Europe on this form of abuse has increased during recent years, in particular, since the late 2000s. In spite of this growth in activism, the prevalence rates present a concerning picture, as do the attrition rates for prosecuting this form of criminal behaviour. On a global basis, the problem of GBV continues unabated. GBV has a negative impact on the well-being of women across the life cycle. Young women are particularly impacted by specific forms of GBV, for example, harassment in public spaces, with 86 per cent (aged 18–24) in the UK reporting that they have been sexually harassed in a public space (APPG for UN Women, 2021). Young women also report being abused and harassed online, with one in five in the UK reporting this (Ipsos MORI, 2017), in schools (Ofsted, 2021) and at universities (EVAWG, 2021). Young women from ethnic minority backgrounds are more likely to suffer sexual harassment online (Girlguiding, 2021). Though our understanding of this issue has grown over the years, there has been limited attention given to the voices of young women to fully understand their lived experiences.

Among women (aged 18–24), 86 per cent have voiced that they have been sexually harassed in public spaces (11 per cent did not answer the question). Therefore, only 3 per cent did not recall ever having experienced sexually harassing behaviour (APPG for UN Women, 2021). US evidence indicates that approximately one in 11 young women experience physical abuse, with one in eight reporting having experienced sexual abuse and 26 per cent reporting experiencing stalking (CDC, 2021). The UK figures from the Crime Survey for England and Wales illustrate the extent of the problem, with an estimated 1.6 million adults (aged 16–74) reporting having experienced sexual assault by rape or penetration (including attempts) since the age of 16, with less than one in six reporting the crime to the police (ONS, 2021). The Crime Survey for England and Wales understates the problem, as not all forms of abuse are captured; nor is consideration given to patterns of repeated intimate partner violence. In the UK, one in four women will experience domestic abuse (ONS, 2021), with a reduced global figure of one in three (WHO, 2021). The picture becomes even bleaker when considering that this form of abuse is 'hidden' and stigmatised, with associated barriers to reporting these crimes. On a global basis, the COVID-19 pandemic has had a devasting impact on the prevalence rates of domestic abuse. For example, during the initial stages of the pandemic, Australian data indicated that almost 10 per cent of women in a relationship had experienced domestic violence during the pandemic (Boxall, Morgan and Brown, 2020), while US evidence also reflects an increasing trend in domestic violence (Boserup, McKenney and Elkbull, 2020). The United Nations evidence reflects the devasting and relentless impact of violence against women and girls, with an estimated daily count of 137 women killed by their intimate partner or a family member (United Nations, 2019).

Levels of abuse on the surface appear comparable for both young men and women, masking the deeper impact of abusive behaviour patterns on female well-being, and subsequently disguising the true gender divide. Young women use violence defensively (Stark, 2007), with young men constructing their masculinity based on violence perpetrated (Totten, 2003). Women and young women are subjected to more abuse than men when the frequency, severity, range and impact of the abuse is considered (Foshee, 1996; Molidor and Tolman, 1998; WHO, 2005; Stark, 2007; Humphreys et al, 2008; Barter et al, 2009; Wood et al, 2011; Radford et al, 2011). Explanations of the higher prevalence of younger women experiencing GBV revolves around societal perceptions about their current generation. It is perceived that younger women tend to have a greater number of intimate partners than older women, are vulnerable to physical male strength, are more financially dependent than older women and are generally more vulnerable due to their child-rearing role (Jewkes et al, 2014).

The nature of young intimate relationships has shifted significantly, as 'online' relationships and the emergence of the new media technologies play a key role in perpetuating gendered norms and patterns of coercion and control within these relationships (Ringrose, 2012). Significant concerns have also been identified regarding the coercive nature of teenage relationships and the confusion between 'caring' and 'controlling' behaviour (Barter et al, 2009), with particular practices such as 'sexting' and the non-consensual circulation of images, reflecting wider gendered sexual pressures. Young women are subject to sexual 'double standards', whereby sexually active young men are labelled as the 'norm' and sexually active young women are stigmatised or labelled in a derogatory manner as 'slags/sluts' (Ringrose et al, 2012).

Current debates continue to highlight the gaps in education focused on promoting healthy relationships, in particular, the lack of teaching the importance of 'sexual consent' and 'respect' within young people's intimate relationships.

The nature and patterns of abuse

The pattern of abuse within young people's relationships parallels adult intimate partner abuse, in that it exists on a continuum, extending from verbal and emotional abuse to sexual assault and murder. As discussed in later chapters, there are also key differences in the nature, patterns and visibility of abuse in young intimate relationships in comparison with adult relationships. Key concerns focus on the presence of this abuse across online and offline communities (Ringrose et al, 2012; Barter et al, 2015). Indeed, survivors of teenage domestic abuse are twice as likely to have sent a sexual image or message, compared with young people who have not been victimised (Barter et al, 2015). The impact of domestic abuse on pregnant young women is under-researched in the UK; however, the available research demonstrates higher levels of risk of abuse for them (Rosen, 2004; Schutt, 2006; Wood et al, 2011). Research has begun to explore this complex issue further, and reflects links with 'coerced sex' (Wood and Barter, 2015), sexual pressure, sexual negotiations and autonomy. Gang activity also exacerbates the presence and risk of domestic abuse, including sexual exploitation and coerced criminal behaviour (Berelowitz et al, 2012).

In order to begin to contextualise and address these concerns, there needs to be a focus on the wider nature and pattern of behaviour within young intimate relationships, and the progression of these relationships, specifically, an exploration of courtship or dating norms. The interviews with the young women concentrated on the progression of their intimate relationships, including exploring the beginning of their relationships and the course of them, the nature of their relationships, the role of social media within relationships and their views on support and information available on intimate relationships. Open-ended questions were used to allow participants the space to describe their experiences of established intimate relationships, 'going out' with someone and also 'going on dates'. In order to provide a sense of the relationship experiences of the sample group, across the sample, 60 per cent (15) of the young women interviewed had direct experience of being in an intimate relationship. For many of the young women, the relationship they were describing was their first intimate one, with none of the relationships involving child-rearing/parenting or cohabitation. One relationship involved a step-parenting role and staying over at the boyfriend's home during weekends, as he was older and had his own home.

Based on my recollection of relationship experiences within my own peer group, I anticipated that the duration of most of the relationships would be within the timescale of a couple of months (Carver et al, 2003). However, the discussions with the young women revealed that over half of their relationships had lasted longer than a few months, with several of them lasting beyond a year. This does link to the age of the sample, as the majority of the young women with direct relationship experience were over the age of 16 (13 of the 15 young women), which aligns with research which reflects that relationship experience and average relationship duration develops with age (Meier and Allen, 2009). All the relationships were described as heterosexual. The remaining 40 per cent of the sample (ten young women) reflected on their peer or family intimate relationships (primarily siblings) and the vignettes. Despite the limited relationship experience of this portion of the sample, these young women drew upon their observations of their peers, their experiences of gender norms and their wider experiences of harassment/'catcalling' within their school and wider public spaces. As illustrated later, the young women with no or limited relationship experience were generally more reflective of theirselves and their relationship expectations.

From the relationships described, 83 per cent featured some form of harmful behaviour; however, not all behaviours were identified as 'harmful' or abusive by the young women. The presence of emotional harm was the most visible, which underpinned and sustained wider harmful behaviours in all these cases, as well as appearing as a form of isolated harm. This was closely followed by overt verbal abuse, coercive controlling behaviour and online patterns of abuse. The coercive controlling behaviour also included sexual coercion and threatening behaviour. There were no explicit examples of financial abuse or direct physical harm. This harmful behaviour, in particular, verbal abuse and controlling behaviour, often played out within the public sphere, within view of, or at least in the knowledge of, their peers and often also their family members. This may be due to the routine of the daily contact of young people within large mixed gender groups in school and other learning environments. This is in sharp contrast to the 'hidden' nature of adult domestic abuse, as this remains an unseen and highly stigmatised issue within more mature relationships (HMIC, 2014; Women's Aid, 2017; ONS, 2021).

The interview data indicated that the most common form of abuse experienced by the young women in the sample group was emotional harm. For this purpose, emotional abuse is defined as including a continuum of behaviour perceived as abusive and harmful, as well as verbal abuse, and threatening and controlling behaviour. As with similar research, some young women described mutually occurring emotional abuse (Barter et al, 2009; Barter et al, 2015). However, the nature and impact of the emotional abuse perpetrated and experienced by these women were different and more severe than their boyfriends'. While there are examples within this research of emotional abuse mutually occurring, the young women spoke of their emotional and verbal abuse as being reactive to their boyfriends' behaviour. Therefore, young men were primarily the instigators of emotional harm within the context of their intimate relationship. Though these conclusions are drawn based on interviews with young women, research demonstrates that young men overestimate the degree of abuse they experience as part of their intimate relationships (Lavoie et al, 2000; Barter et al, 2009). This could have been due to the nature of this sample, as young women are the group most at risk of this form of abuse, and the fact that the focus of this research was on creating a female-only space to discuss experiences.

The emotional impact of a spectrum of abuse on young women was a key thread across the interviews. For many young women, this meant experiencing abuse online, offline or on the street, as well as within an intimate relationship. The participants demonstrated a high level of 'everyday' contact with harassment and abuse, with evidence of incidences escalating into violent behaviour. The majority of participants knew of someone in their family, peer group or the wider community who had suffered harassment, abuse or violence. The focus is on identifying the context in which young women recounted experiences of abuse within their intimate relationships, with particular attention given to the influence of gendered social norms and the continuum of abuse experienced, rather than a binary focus on whether abuse is justified or seen as unacceptable behaviour.

Coercive control and 'his mood'

As previously outlined, the theoretical position adopted here is a feminist perspective with a focus on structural power inequities based on the unequal social construction of gender that favours masculinity. Therefore, domestic abuse within intimate relationships is explained as the consequence of power and control by men over women due to the wider social, structural and institutional inequities. Coercive control as a form of abuse falls within this definition and is described as a pattern of intimidation, isolation and control used by men in order to limit women's autonomy, again as a result of structural inequalities (Stark, 2007). Stark discusses the concept of coercive control in relation to freedom and oppression within an analogy of the 'invisible cage'. He describes how movements are policed, even when women are attempting to undertake everyday routine tasks, in order to limit personal space and choice with the aim of creating complete isolation (p 366). Through the total dominance and emotional control of every aspect of women's lives, they experience their personal life as if they were living in a cage as prisoners (p 199). Williamson (2010) highlights the importance of critically evaluating the coercive and controlling aspects of abuse to ensure that the impact on a woman's identity and sense of self is realistically understood and addressed.

The closeness of a school environment impacts on the surveillance of young people by their abusers (Lagerlöf and Øverlien, 2022). The presence of surveillance, restricting movements and limiting decisions, was commonplace throughout the narratives shared by the young women. The abusive behaviour described often triggered other forms of abuse, in particular, verbal abuse, humiliation and sexual coercion. The pattern of control discussed earlier illustrates a drive towards isolation, focused on limiting social freedom and severing friendships. The influence of 'his mood' in dictating the relationship landscape was evident throughout several of the narratives. The switch in 'his mood' was seen as an indicator of his dissatisfaction with a decision, and a trigger for a limitation to the choices to be made. 'His mood' also changed in response to jealousy and paranoia, and was a sign of increased control in order to limit contact with friends and family. However, while explicitly discussing their acknowledgement of this mood change, and indeed their dislike of its consequences, its impact was minimised by some of the young women and responses were framed as a "fear of losing them [their boyfriends]". This was irrespective of the build-up towards an argument "if he's in a mood", or the realisation of the reason behind his behaviour. As Michelle explained:

'I wanted to go with my friends on New Year's Eve. I wanted to look at the option of splitting the evening between him and my friends – he "got in a mood" and said that he was not happy and placed a sad face on "my story" on Snapchat. I changed my plans with my friends; once he got his own way, he was OK.' (Michelle)

Michelle described the control in their relationship, which essentially led to her boyfriend having his own way to avoid him "being in a mood". In several instances, control was focused on dictating social contact with friends:

'He wouldn't let me go and see my friends, only in the evenings. If I saw them lunchtime, then he would go off in a mood. He expected me to stay with him lunchtimes. My friends would say, "You need to leave him or you won't have anyone", but I didn't listen, I lost them in the end but I got them back.' (Lowri)

Again, 'his mood' played a key part in triggering controlling behaviour and limiting Lowri's movements as if she was within an 'invisible cage'. Peers were often influential in triggering arguments and abusive outbursts:

'He would also accuse me of talking with other boys on social media … I would get upset and stay quiet. At the end of the day, he would come up to me and apologise as his friends had said that they had been joking. His friends would get in his head.' (Lowri)

The fear and threat of using social media to not only monitor movements but also humiliate and punish young women was evident. This overt display of abusive behaviour is contrary to the hidden nature of adult abusive behaviours, indicating a lack of awareness of acceptable behaviours or the need to hide this harmful display. This was particularly evident when young women attended social events, contrary to their boyfriends' wishes. This would often result in extended periods of "mood", control and surveillance.

When attending social gatherings or parties by themselves, there was a general description of a specific line of constant questioning at the pre-party stage, described as, "Why can't I come?", "Who else will be there?", "Where's the party?" While the party was in full flow, they described receiving multiple messages and phone calls and, post-party, one young woman described being questioned by her boyfriend two weeks after the event. The result of going against his wishes was further surveillance via multiple calls/text messages and automatic accusations, as explained by Rhiannon: "If I was doing something with my friends, I would get loads of missed calls – he would ask, 'are you with boys?', 'no', 'don't lie to me'". The reply offered to the constant questioning would not be satisfactory, often leading to unfounded accusations. Jealousy was described as a key trigger for most arguments, with peer groups and friends often taking centre stage. Chloe described how the boys within her year group would often come up to her and place their arms around her to spite and spark a reaction from her boyfriend, who was a year older. Not only does this illustrate the attitude towards women as items to possess but it also reinforces the notion of striving to be the hegemonic male. The culturally and socially accepted response to this behaviour is to trigger a jealous reaction, and reclaim Chloe in a public manner by performing this specific role. Her boyfriend would get angry and blame her for the explicit behaviour of the young men within her peer group. This was despite her request to "blame them, not me". Chloe went on to describe how this behaviour had subsided as her boyfriend "trusts her now", but the reality was that he was no longer a witness to this behaviour as he had left school.

Aleysha described the power imbalance in her relationship with an older male, perpetuated by their age gap, role and responsibilities. This power differential was further exacerbated by her reaction to his reputation as a serial womaniser. When she went out with her friends, he decided when she returned home, as he would collect her in his car. A rejection of his offer would commence a line of questioning focused on "who's giving you a lift? or where are you staying then?" She felt that this established routine resulted in his power over her social arrangements, her movements and when she returned home. However, she had no control over when he returned home after a night out, and would attempt to address this by staying up all night to await his phone call or his return to stay at her home. Again, this reinforced his position of power, which was justified and naturalised by her belief that "boys want to be in control and they decide", with any reaction to his behaviour as a result of her going into "psychotic girlfriend mode". Aleysha's strategy to respond to his control was self-blame through the use of established gendered norms and the stereotype of the "psycho girlfriend". While she was in the self-blame mode, his position was reinforced by his reputation as a womaniser, which empowered his status. This further placed her in a difficult position of whether she was rational to withdraw trust. She also felt that if she did not have sex with him, her role within the relationship would become redundant.

The findings align with previous research, which suggests that young people are less likely than adults to recognise emotional harm and control experienced within their intimate relationships (Lavoie at al, 2000; Chung, 2005; Barter et al, 2009). Abusive behaviour was less excused by those young women who had left abusive relationships, which aligns with previous findings (Barter et al, 2009). The women who did acknowledge abusive behaviour understood the consequences of the abuse, resulting in less justification or categorisation of behaviour as permissible. This linked to their subsequent understanding of the impact of a continuum of behaviour, which filtered through all aspects of their offline and online lives, to the detriment of their well-being.

Sexual coercion and abuse

The confusion of young women in attempting to identify their own experiences of sexual harm and exploitation is linked to a misunderstanding of consensual and non-consensual sex. Due to gendered pressures and sexual coercion, young women have limited power to negotiate sexual contact and consent. As explained by Sieg (2000), researchers have continually illustrated the challenges faced by these women in developing positive sexual identities within the 'regimes of youth regulation' (Rattansi and Phoenix, 1997). Normative gendered attitudes continue to shape the landscape for young intimate relationships, including the pressure on young women to be passive and appear like a 'Barbie doll', which aligns with the perception of the male notion of attractiveness.

There remains a visible conflict between the concept of sexual knowingness and experience on the one hand, and the expectations of girlhood as innocence on the other. Society positions young women as either active sexual beings or passive, with the complex sexual subjectivities of young women more complicated than this static binary (Ringrose and Renold,

2012). Dominant constructions of young female sexuality have only served to perpetuate the sexual commodification of young women and the false promise of sexual liberation packaged as 'girl power' (Coy, 2013). In reality, any form of sexual liberation is subject to shaming, with the aim of reversing any perceived sense of sexual freedom. Ultimately, young women learn to restrict themselves, specifically, with regard to their physical appearance and sexual choices. The narratives illustrated their limited choices and dilemma, either of becoming sexually restrained or overtly sexually active, both polar extremes. There were also examples of young women who elected to be sexually active within their relationships; however, this information was often well established within their peer group. How this information was conceptualised and shared was at the mercy of their peer group or close friends. Their perceived available space was to be passive and preserve their appearance, and essentially their reputation, in a 'subtle' manner, to become invisible and avoid the label of slut/slag or to openly share their photos, information and sexual experiences. This notion of abstinence was cloaked as being 'subtle', as sexuality and sex were conceptualised as 'dirty' and unhealthy. Those who did elect to be "subtle" were mostly those not actively within relationships, not engaging in social media discussions or not invited to attend social events. Narratives revealed that some of the young women felt that they lost respect for themselves and that they lost respect from young men following sex: "I didn't respect myself then ... sex means a lot, but for some boys, it's not – it's just a shag" (Aleysha). There is a suggestion that respect is related to sexual actions and peer judgement, illustrating the continued pressure on young women to be vigilant of themselves and others.

There was a sense of urgency in the way the young women sought out acceptance and advice about their sexual actions from me as an independent researcher. Overall, there was a sense of pressing need to discuss their sexual experiences on a one-to-one basis within the confidential context of a research interview, in particular, their first sexual experience. In part, this illustrated a lack of space for young women to talk freely and ask advice about their sexuality and sex without the fear of judgement and repercussions. The dichotomy of presenting their body in a 'subtle' manner to avoid judgement and the need to be attractive/desirable served as a barrier to seeking adult guidance. This also often occurred within the context of unwanted male attention and harassment. The ethical obligation to preserve their privacy made this a safe place to discuss their experiences and views. Young women modified their behaviour to avoid judgement, while they described how young men navigated a position of pressure to overtly expose their sexualised actions. As illustrated by Bonnie, Delyth and Jennifer, "Boys are 'bang, bang, all about sex'" (Bonnie), "Guys are legends for having sex, it's like, 'let's see how many girls we can sleep with'" (Jennifer) and "Girls tend to talk about arguments and boys are more laid back and talk more about who they have slept with – boys are more reserved" (Delyth). Collette and Lowri describe the gendered pressure and expectations: "There's more pressure on boys to 'get in there' cos they just want to 'do it' and lose their virginity" (Collette, 16 years old) and "There's more pressure on girls to have sex. If girls say 'no' it causes arguments and if girls continue to say 'no', they will break up with you and find someone" (Lowri). While young women should remain 'subtle', it was seen as a normative expectation that young men would be 'up for' sex all the time and would modify their behaviour to 'get it'.

Participants reflected the importance of privacy of their sexual choices and the repercussions of judgement when information was openly disclosed. Young women are faced with an impossible task of avoiding judgement at both ends of the spectrum, whether they participate in or withdraw from sexual activities. Michelle was pressurised to have sex with a young man she wanted a relationship with, and when she thought "fair enough" and had sex with him, he later refused to establish a relationship with her. Michelle's experience of losing her virginity illustrates limited female agency. The knowledge of their sexual relations was shared around the school, which resulted in derogatory remarks shouted across the classroom: "I just laugh it off. It makes me angry, but I try to laugh it off" (Michelle). Michelle reflects on her limited agency and space to challenge these remarks and demonstrate her anger. She therefore resorted to humour in an attempt to brush the comments to one side as a method of pretending that this does not impact on her. As this information became "common knowledge" across the school, her friends became aware and appeared "shocked" and disappointed by her behaviour. This demonstrates a degree of victim blaming and a sense of judgement that Michelle deserved the consequences of her actions, as she had "chosen" to be used for sex, further perpetuating the culture and limited space to challenge this form of behaviour. The commentary and judgement by her friends were focused solely on Michelle's sexual activity, which is a form of 'slut shaming' that labels her choice and behaviour, with no repercussion or focus on the young man's behaviour. This reinforces the claustrophobic environments of schools that Lagerlöf and Øverlien (2002) explored, with a particular focus on both the restrictions within the school routine, which can often perpetuate abusive behaviour, and the social exclusion experienced as a result of peer reactions to harassment. Being in the same class as an abuser has also been identified as a key barrier to ending a relationship (Korkmaz, 2021).

The internal conflict experienced by participants was evident through their narratives, body language and in the urgent need they conveyed to discuss the acceptability of their decision making, in particular, regarding their first sexual experience. The often unspoken dilemma of their decision-making process of agreeing or disagreeing to have sex was a key theme weaving throughout their narratives. However, the consequences of their potential refusal to have sex were overtly known and questioned: "What if they don't like me if I don't 'do it?'" (Rhiannon) and "When you say 'no', they say 'fuck off then' if you're not going to do that" (Aleysha). The consequences of refusing sexual consent were framed in the aggression of the language used. This was further confirmed by the message that "If you don't have sex with them, they won't want you" (Aleysha). This rejection and coercion was overtly conveyed by a change in mood and character of their boyfriends as they would either 'get in a mood' or 'sulk' if they faced a rejection or a refusal of their sexual advances. Elen's experience reflects her boyfriend as the instigator, manipulator and coercer of sexual intercourse:

Elen: He would decide everything. He would make the first move.
Interviewer: How did you feel you could respond?
Elen: I was really scared the first time, obviously. With time I just thought, ugh.
Interviewer: If you couldn't be bothered, what would happen?
Elen: He would sulk and then go to sleep.
Interviewer: Did you stay over and in the same bedroom?
Elen: My dad was like, oh my God – my mum was okay about it and just thought it would happen anyway – at least it's in his house.
Interviewer: Did you feel pressure to have sex with him as you were in the routine of sleeping in his house?
Elen: Yes, I suppose and I didn't want him to sulk.
Interviewer: What would him sulking mean?
Elen: Every time he would sulk, it would make me feel bad – I just wanted to please him. I think that's why I felt low. If we didn't have sex, then he would sulk, so we would have sex.

Across a continuum of behaviour, the analysis of Elen's experience reflects the common features of emotionally harmful and coercive behaviour, in particular, the unequal power relations within young intimate relationships and the dominance of young women by young men. The overall construction of female sexuality conformed to heterosexual norms of passivity, as the desires of their boyfriends were perceived as paramount, their own desires being of secondary importance. For example, Chloe demonstrates her confusion and concern about the potential judgement from her peers, her self-blame of not feeling ready to have sex and primary concern of what she saw as the impact on her boyfriend of not knowing "where he stood":

'I was resigned to the idea of sex after a period of seven months – "do it with the right person". I was worried what they [her friends] would think ... its important to me what they thought ... I had previously said that I wasn't ready, then said that I was more ready to progress the relationship. The uncertainty meant that he didn't know where he stood.' (Chloe)

The fact that she felt "resigned" to having sex reflects that she felt it was a duty to have sex at this time, essentially, that as the relationship and time progressed, that this was an expectation on her as a girlfriend. Reflections on the research journal notes that Chloe's body language became closed and guarded as she described how she felt "resigned" to having sex. Chloe also voices the dilemma of pleasing her boyfriend, despite her concern of being judged by her peers, with her wishes and desires secondary to this concern. The consequences of coercion, both subtly and overtly, resulted in participants questioning their self-worth and character if they submitted to both unwanted and wanted advances. This illustrates the requirement of responding positively to male sexual demands, with the sanctions of refusing to respond to their needs well known and rehearsed. The worth of being a good/bad girlfriend was also measured by physical appearance and sexual performance: "Boys look at bums and having boobs and are they [girls] good in bed" (Bonnie). Furthermore, participants questioned the uncharted territory of first sexual experiences, "taking a step back" once the realm of sexual activity had been entered, and several perceived norms of young sexual relationships. Young men were, on the surface, seen as sexually confident: "Boys are more confident to discuss sex – girls think more about the consequences; boys think about the 'moment'" (Chloe); while Chloe was concerned about whether she had made the right decision to have sex and "had to take a step back" after the event, she questioned whether once she had sex, did she always have to have sex now? Not only does this illustrate the structural pressures but also the pressures within relationships and the uncertainty of the boundaries around sex, choice and control. Gender norms formed the bedrock of the young women's understanding of their sexualisation, sexual identity and agency to select when to have sex. Their narratives revealed the role of gender as pivotal to their understanding of their role within intimate relationships.

Physical violence and abuse

Arguments were generally normalised as acceptable within intimate relationships; however, a line was drawn when the arguments became physical or threatening, with an acknowledgement that this was unacceptable.

This reflected a traditional belief of abuse as physical violence. There were several examples of boyfriends approaching their girlfriends and shouting abuse close in their face, invading personal space and causing fear. "He would shout in my face and that would make me feel uncomfortable. But when he said 'sorry', that would mean a lot to me" (Lowri). Despite the advice from Lowri's friends that her boyfriend was "nasty", she justified his behaviour and was reassured by his constant apologising. This was despite his actions of frequently humiliating her in front of her peers, with examples of explicit verbal abuse within the school grounds during break and lunchtimes. However, peers were often influential in triggering arguments and abusive outbursts:

> 'He would also accuse me of talking with other boys on social media ... I would get upset and stay quiet. At the end of the day, he would come up to me and apologise as his friends had said that they had been joking. His friends would get in his head.' (Lowri)

The escalation of controlling and verbal abuse was focused on the physical display of "his mood", with his temper escalating with a physical outburst to damage property and objects, as illustrated by Bonnie.

Interviewer:	How did he generally treat you?
Bonnie:	I don't know. He was alright, yeah. But I know he did lose his temper a lot, yeah.
Interviewer:	If he lost his temper, how would he show that?
Bonnie:	Punching things.
Interviewer:	Just go round punching things?
Bonnie:	Yeah. I just said, what is the point? You're going to regret that in about half an hour, when you've got to clean up all the glass and everything. I wouldn't clean it for him. You made it, you can clean it.
Interviewer:	So he would just get angry, then he'd go round punching things in the house?
Bonnie:	Yeah.
Interviewer:	How would that make you feel?
Bonnie:	I don't know. I just used to laugh at him in my head, yeah. Like, what is the point? You've got a punching bag outside, yeah, go punch that. I'd just laugh at him.
Interviewer:	Did you ever feel uncomfortable?
Bonnie:	When he got mad, yeah.
Interviwer:	What would he do then when you started to feel uncomfortable?
Bonnie:	Just go to a different room and smash there instead.

There was a sense of 'calmness' voiced by the young women placed in these types of circumstances, including an understanding that this form of behaviour was to be expected in certain circumstances. Closer examination would also suggest that this calmness was a lack of control or power to divert the situation or the escalation in behaviour. And the justification and naturalisation of this behaviour:

> 'He stormed out punching the walls – he has a short behaviour anger thing. He had a bad day at work and *I was provoking him*. I just thought, "what are you doing?" I've seen it with my older brother, for some girls it would have been more scary, but I've seen it before. *You have to meet their needs and their wants.'* (Aleysha, emphasis her own)

Aleysha describes how her boyfriend physically displays his anger and excuses his behaviour as a "short behaviour anger thing", due to his "bad day at work" and her perception of self-blame that she was "provoking him". She justifies his behaviour and blames herself, while explaining that this is natural male behaviour that she has witnessed with her brother, again reinforcing her belief that this is acceptable and natural. Her self-blame extends further to illustrate her coping mechanism when she claims that there is a requirement to "meet their wants and needs" and failure to do so therefore has consequences. This resolution of damaging or throwing items was common, and often justified as a male behaviour trait triggered by his mood, temper and tendency to sulk: "He would throw items ... he threw a crutch across the room when I tried to finish things" (Elen). Elen was visibly upset when she was revisiting the end of this relationship. His physical response to her wish to end their relationship illustrates the tendency for physical violence and abuse to escalate at the end or following the end of an intimate relationship when the woman attempts to sever his control and he attempts to regain his power (Mahoney, 1991).

The shame and stigma of being in a "bad relationship" is also apparent as "I don't know because with most people, if they are in one of them bad relationships, they don't exactly talk about it, no. Just like, yeah, yeah, we're okay" (Bonnie). Bonnie illustrates the pressure of the work of managing her emotions to hide her true feelings, due to the norm of 'not talking about it' and the belief of not being believed. The pressure to present a picture of a 'perceived ideal relationship' is evident. This presentation is maintained until the epiphany moment leading to the end of their abusive relationships. For example, for Bonnie, it was the "smashing" of items in front of her and then his subsequent disappearance which made her realise that his behaviour was unacceptable. For Elen, it was the persistent name calling and the observation from a new friend that this behaviour was unacceptable. For Lowri, it was the public name calling that resulted in her sharing her concerns with her father, who subsequently intervened. However, for some, this symbolic point of change was yet to occur (for example, Aleysha).

Reflections

Across the discussion of experiences of abuse, emotional abuse and coercive control resulted in a general negative impact on well-being, in particular, self-confidence. Elen described that her long-term boyfriend would "call me a 'slag/harlot' … I felt low, I lost my confidence, I didn't know how to finish things". Often, the emotional and verbal abuse escalated further, with the threat of physical harm evident, and resulted in a negative impact on the young women's well-being: "I felt alone and stupid" (Elen). Elen illustrates the negative impact of having limited access to support as a young woman isolated in an abusive relationship:

Interviewer: How was your relationship?
Elen: He planted stuff in my mind about my friends. I wasn't that well, so I would go home often. I slowly lost contact with my friends and I would stop getting invites to stuff. I was with him in break and lunchtime. I was manipulated so I couldn't see my friends. He would stop me or say no – he would just make me feel guilty and manipulate the situation. If I wanted to go out with one my friends, this was at the end; I had decided that I didn't want to be on my own. He would text me and say, "why are you with her, she's a slag, guaranteed you are doing stuff like what she does, you're going to be like her. You will end up like her". He would text me or phone me to get me off work (I worked in a pub doing karaoke).
Interviewer: Why did he call her a slag?
Elen: Actually, I don't know as she's a virgin. I just didn't listen to him. She got really angry about this as well and texted him back to tell him to let leave me alone. It started with little things that he would say, I just didn't realise. I realised when I noticed I had no friends left. I really noticed this when I was with my friend and I could see things clearer. I think it was really good that she was there – she would say "this is not right" – she offered me advice and support.

Elen describes how she was manipulated and how the feelings of guilt isolated her from her friends. However, she highlights the importance of having support, the power of having the reflections of an outsider on the negative behaviour, that her friends "got really angry" and thought that his behaviour was "not right". As a result of these reflections, advice and support, she was able to realise the patterns of abusive behaviour and the impact of this on her well-being and access to friendship/support. The impact on the young women's overall identity and sense of self was also evident: "He made me a more nervous person – I was 'in my shell' and more reserved … I'm glad it's over – I'm now a different person now it's finished" (Delyth). There was evident relief when a relationship finally ended and they could reclaim their agency: "I feel more confident, I'm now the person I was before and I'm more outgoing" (Delyth).

It was evident that young women who were currently involved in an intimate relationship tended to be less critical of their current relationship, in comparison with past experiences. Consideration needs to be given to enhancing the protective factor of young women, not only to provide protection but to educate them on identifying the signs and symptoms of abusive behaviour. While understanding risk and protective factors is vital when assessing needs and support, it is important to reiterate that the key aim is to prevent violence and abuse through a zero-tolerance approach. This is the preferred option, rather than identifying and evaluating perceived risk and vulnerability factors or working to modify the behaviour of young women by adopting a protectionist approach. The responsibility for this form of abuse should always remain with the abuser.

3

Gender norms and young intimate relationship roles

Existing research on young intimate relationships often neglects to draw upon the ways in which attitudes and gender norms shape the embodiment of gendered roles for young people. While it is acknowledged that the research here builds on previous research on young intimate relationships, the focus is on addressing the gaps in evidence on exploring the progression of young intimate relationships. Research has focused on 'dating violence and abuse', 'hooking up' (Bogle, 2008) or the impact of social media on dating norms, rather than the progression of intimate relationships or the impact of gender norms on the ritual of forming romantic and intimate relationships. The aim of this research was to engage with young women who have been in intimate relationships, and those who are yet to encounter these experiences, in order to gain a more nuanced picture of their attitudes towards their gender, normative expectations and perception and experiences of relationships from both these perspectives, essentially, examining the overall structural link to the normative social construction of gender in our society today.

For young people, intimate relationships, 'going out', relationship exclusivity, 'courtship' or 'dating' morph into different forms depending on several factors, such as local norms, age group and peers. Young people begin initiating intimate relationships during early adolescence, between the ages of 10 and 13 (Stonard et al, 2015; Davies, 2019). Young intimate relationships differ from adult relationships, specifically with regards to the role expectations, the degree of intimacy, the duration and everyday routines (Hickman et al, 2004; Davies, 2019). The discussion ahead will focus on the gendered social construction of intimate relationships, basically, the norm or cultural feature of courtship, specifically, the perceived benefits and comfort gained from accepting established gendered scripts, rather than suffering the consequences of non-conformity. The young women interviewed expressed a lack of power to operationalise their egalitarian attitudes in order to engage in relationships that adhere to the description of what they expect, want or desire within a 'healthy relationship'. As a default position, they relied and drew upon normative scripts, and concentrated primarily on essentialist beliefs. This resulted in the young women undertaking daily 'impression management' of performing both the 'doing of gender' and the perceived 'ideal girlfriend' role, often to their own detriment. It will be argued that barriers preventing the operationalisation of their attitudes, beliefs, wishes and feelings reinforce gender differences, providing unstable grounding for a change towards 'real' gender equality. The chapter will conclude by highlighting that young women perform what they see as the expected girlfriend role to satisfy the needs of their audience, essentially, to maintain what Goffman termed as 'facework' (Goffman, 1955), to pay 'lip service' to their boyfriends' demands to the detriment of their own self-development of identity.

Gendered norms and attitudes

A norm is conceptualised as a belief embraced by the majority within a community and can be identified as an actual, perceived or misperceived norm. Social norms can influence attitudes and behaviours on an individual and community level (Berkowitz, 2012). The importance of investigating the relationship between social norms, attitudes and abusive behaviour is evident (Price and Byers, 1999; Flood and Pease, 2009) in order to gauge whether attitudes reflect the ideas of abusive behaviour on a continuum of interlinked 'everyday experiences' or as episodic incidents. Community attitudes are a significant factor in helping us understand the perpetration of violence and abuse against women (Flood and Pease, 2009), evaluate community and institutional responses to this 'hidden issue', identify power dynamics and understand how to challenge this issue.

The traditional role of young women within intimate relationships has been associated with passivity and respectability (Connell, 1987). The normative socialisation of young women enforces the idea of males as 'strong' and 'in control' and females as 'weak' and 'compliant', reinforcing gendered responsibility within relationships. Our understanding of how young women conceptualise their role, identity and abusive behaviour within their own intimate relationships is limited, as is our knowledge of the implications of this behaviour on their well-being. Normative gendered attitudes threaten the development of self-determination and limit sexual desires and, indeed, the role of young women. As a result, gendered expectations and social norms impact on attitudes and stereotypes, with these women facing pressures to negotiate an appropriate level of engagement in sexualised behaviour while continuing to conform to unrealistic body image standards, while young men have pressure to conform to heterosexual standards of sexualised behaviour or face being labelled as 'gay' or lacking masculinity (Zero Tolerance, 2014). Analysing young women's attitudes can assist us in understanding gendered 'scripts', the social stereotypes perpetuating these scripts and the reinforcement of them by young people. Focusing on the attitudes of participants of abuse in different contexts (for example, with the use of vignettes) was pertinent; as Reinharz explains, 'we cannot understand the *meaning* of behaviour without knowing the attitudes behind it' (1992, p 85).

Young women's attitudes to abuse and dating

There is well-documented evidence on the continuing presence of gendered sexist attitudes to the acceptability of violence and abuse in certain circumstances (Burton and Kitzinger, 1998; Burman and Cartmel, 2005; Lacasse and Mendelson, 2007; Powell and Webster, 2018). A key theme explored as part of this research was the young women's attitudes towards patterns of behaviour and the particular justifications for these behaviours. From the analysis of the data, it is possible to draw some conclusions regarding their attitudes towards overtly abusive behaviour and coercive control. Over 82.3 per cent of participants agreed that there was 'never a reason for a boyfriend to threaten their girlfriends', with only 10.5 per cent disagreeing with this statement. This overarching attitude condemning the abuse of young women was further echoed in the response, as 90 per cent of participants agreed that 'boyfriends should not damage their girlfriends' belongings'. There was recognition that threatening behaviour as a whole was unacceptable, including the wider spectrum of abuse beyond direct violence. Despite this acknowledgement, over half of the participants agreed that 'sometimes boyfriends cannot help but swear at their girlfriends'. This indicates that threatening behaviour and behaviour focusing on damaging property were regarded as unacceptable, while verbal abuse was perceived as justifiable, with less than 30 per cent of participants disagreeing with this notion.

Overwhelmingly, not a single participant agreed with the statement in the survey that it was 'OK for boyfriends to use private information to make girlfriends do something'. Other forms of controlling behaviour, such as selecting friends, sexual coercion and financial control, were overwhelmingly regarded as 'not OK'. Just over 30 per cent of participants agreed that a boyfriend who texted and phoned all day was 'just being caring', with 30 per cent noting that they 'didn't know', illuminating some of the challenges of unpicking the nuanced nature of controlling behaviour. This was further illustrated when participants were asked to respond 'yes' or 'no' to whether they saw particular behaviours as abusive. The several forms of justifications offered in response to violent behaviour, mainly the act of 'slapping', were overwhelmingly rejected. While this gave a clear indication of the unacceptability of various excuses, from retaliation, jealousy, intoxication and apologising after the event, the idea of whether these particular attitudes operationalised into their everyday relationships was a key theme explored further in the interviews, in particular, as the questionnaire responses offered a firm rejection of these forms of justifications. In keeping with the notion of a continuum of abuse, unwanted groping/touching was regarded as harmful by 75 per cent of the participants.

Overall, the response of the sample of young women was consistent in challenging social norms focused on the breadwinner/professional male role and the wife/caring female role. They illustrated attitudes challenging social stereotypes of young women as 'good wives', vulnerable and passive. This challenged the normative belief of women constructed with a dual role: the biological role as child-bearers and the social role as the family member most responsible for undertaking caring tasks. The first three statements on the survey all reflect responses rejecting established attitudes towards social stereotypes, with the disagreement levels for each statement over 80 per cent (83 per cent, 84.5 per cent and 88 per cent), reflecting a consistent disagreement with these beliefs. This level of disagreement shows a progressive approach to traditional social norms; this may be due to the absence of masculinities and the fact that the young women felt at ease to express their views without the ridicule of their male peers within a 'young women-only' space. When exploring attitudes towards particular expectations, the young women responded that it was 'not OK' for it to be expected that girlfriends 'please their boyfriends' to ensure that their relationship 'works', with less than 5 per cent disagreement with this statement. An overwhelming 97 per cent disagreed with the statement that it was 'OK' for boyfriends to 'cheat' while young women should 'always be faithful', with a high level of disagreement of overt statements around 'pleasing' and faithfulness. When exploring ideas around their role in buying 'gifts all the time' or having 'their own way', their answers shifted primarily from the 'strongly disagree' to the 'disagree' category. Despite this, their responses demonstrated attitudes challenging traditional gendered norms.

There was an overwhelming sense (nearly a 90 per cent response) that young men should talk about their feelings, even if others may laugh. These attitudes serve to challenge the established naturalised gender norms focused on the gendered expression of feelings and emotions, and question the reinforced and expected male performance not to be expressive. This aligned with what young women stated they found appealing in a boyfriend, in particular, around the need to be honest about feelings. While there was a general disagreement that young women should care more about their appearance than young men, just over 16 per cent of participants responded 'I don't know' for this question, reflecting a degree of uncertainty on the gendered expectations of physical appearance. However, when questioned on their attitudes towards paying on a date, over half of the sample believed that 'boys should be expected to pay for everything'. Therefore, despite demonstrating a belief that young women could be equal leaders with men, from those surveyed, 38.2 per cent strongly agreed/agreed that men should pay on a date. Not only does this indicate an attitude towards the financial power women pose in relationships but it also demonstrates the actual belief in this power imbalance and their need to be 'cared for'. Participants described the expectation by both parties that young men would pay for 'stuff' on their first date, in particular, the expected norm of paying for dinner, which reflects the view that a good date is measured by the fulfilment of the expectation that the man pays to maintain his control. Most of the young women stated that they did not go on more formal/structured dates until their relationships were more established and had therefore progressed beyond the "cop off" and flirtation stage to the "exclusivity" stage. However, there were dissenting voices illustrating that they felt it was only fair to "split the bill" or "go Dutch". There was an implication that "girls shouldn't expect to be treated" (Chloe), illustrating a view that both blames and distances herself from the perceptions of 'girls':

> 'We shared the bill. He offered initially that he would pay – he brought his card and I brought money. I felt that we should share it. He paid with his card and then I gave him money. That was really important as I wanted to share things as you should do in a relationship. I didn't want to feel as if I was being treated.' (Chloe)

Despite the fact that the bill was shared, Chloe described that she gave him the money afterwards, portraying that, at the point of payment, he performed his masculine role in front of the restaurant staff by acting out and 'managing the impression' of himself as the sole financial provider. The requirement of 'fairness' was seen as a need to be fair towards their male counterparts rather than the fairness of promoting their equal position. There was also a sense that women wanted men to pay for them:

Interviewer: Do you think that young women and young men play different roles within an intimate relationship?

Becky: Definitely, because I think guys like to be more masculine and they like to pay for things and girls tend to just, oh, if you want to pay for things, pay for it, kind of thing. But, in mine, he does do a lot of the paying, but I will, I'll try and contribute, but he'll go, no, I prefer to pay myself. But, yeah, I think there is a bit of a difference, because girls tend to look after the guys more because they tend to need looking after, but guys tend to do more of the, like, sort of masculine side of things.

Across the relationship narratives, the meaning attached to this payment expectation was focused on chivalry; however, this changed as the relationship progressed, with a greater financial expectation then placed on the young women. US research also revealed that men paying on dates was a key part of the dating social script expected by women, in keeping with the 'rules' or traditional rituals of dating. Other key 'rules' of dating for women included acting demure, being feminine and 'playing hard to get' in the sense that a woman should not offer sex on the first three dates (Lamont, 2020). This illustrates the restrictions placed on women, and also by women to restrict their own sexual pleasure and desire in order to align with traditional dating scripts or rules. This also shows the power and static nature of conventional gendered social norms and dating scripts. Adhering to established behaviour patterns avoids the tension, or indeed the outward attention, of considering or following emerging social norms of gender relations. This form of financial expectation relates to norms focused on men as the instigators of the progression of intimate relationships, therefore illustrating the power imbalances at the initial stage of 'dating', including the sense that young men/men do the 'asking out', while women acquiesce, are expected through their appearance to attract male attention and are submissive during the 'date'. This illustrates the contradictory view of modern norms focused on equality, and the traditional norms of 'courtship scripts'. Some narratives offered a degree of resistance to discourses of heteronormative relationships, with dissenting voices questioning the undue pressure on young men to pay. These voices, primarily from those young women with limited direct relationship experience, focused on the importance of establishing egalitarian relationships.

Attitudes influence the images of the perpetrator and victim of violence and abuse, which further reinforces victim-blaming ideas, the social tolerance of specific behaviour and the justification for particular behaviours. Young people may not view abusive behaviour patterns as destructive, in particular, if they are inexperienced or unfamiliar with relationship norms around expectations and boundaries. As discussed later, the need to educate young people on the meaning of gendered norms and abuse, in order to assist in the identification of their experiences as abusive, is evident.

Young women's aspirations for their intimate relationships

The young women were asked to select three items from a list to indicate what they perceived as the most appealing characteristic of a boyfriend and girlfriend. The aim was to identify and compare what they perceived as the most appealing traits for both genders in their role as a boyfriend/girlfriend. The three most popular responses for young men/boyfriends were having a good personality, having a good sense of humour and being honest about feelings, while the key responses for young women/girlfriends were having a good personality, being honest about feelings and having a caring personality. While the key appealing features of having a good personality and being honest about feelings were the same for both genders, men were seen as appealing with a good sense of humour, whereas young women as girlfriends were seen as attractive with a caring personality. This aligned with established social norms of the role of a girlfriend as 'caring', while a boyfriend needed to be fun and have a 'good sense of humour'. This places young women in the 'caring' and passive position of reacting to young men's 'humour' and jokes, resembling the idea of young men as boyish, playful and carefree, while young women are conceptualised as caring and responsible.

Overall, a review of the literature indicates that gender equality, empowered sexual identities, pleasure and desire remain invisible for young women. Narratives of romance position young men as sexually desiring and aggressive, and girls as yearning for love and relationships, which dismisses the importance of women's sexual desire (Fine 1988; Tolman 2002). There was a sense from the young women that attraction was measured by the ability to be in, and have, an intimate relationship, a measure of their heterosexual performance. They revealed the pressure to conform to the perceived ideal image of attractiveness, reinforced by their peers and the online community. There were examples of adapting their appearance and personalities to attract a boyfriend and to maintain their intimate relationship. The young women described how they adopted Goffman's techniques of 'impression management' to stage and maintain their performance as this 'ideal girlfriend'. Goffman (1959) conceptualised 'impression management' as a desire to manipulate our presentation of self to others as part of our social interactions. For example, Chloe described how she wanted the "ideal relationship", which she described as "going out for meals together". This illusion of the "ideal relationship" was shattered in front of her friends when she invited her boyfriend to join them on a trip to the cinema and Pizza Hut. He had "sulked" and refused to talk to anyone:

Interviewer: What made you feel that he didn't want to be there?

Chloe: His body language – he was really quiet and sulked. When I was with my friends, he was more comfortable one to one. He would not talk to me and he argued with me about little things. When I was with my friends, he was more big-headed and showing off, different person really. He made me feel uncomfortable a bit.

Chloe portrayed how she felt uncomfortable and embarrassed due to her boyfriend's behaviour in front of her friends, as he explicitly demonstrated this both verbally and through non-verbal gestures, jeopardising the image she desired to project to her friends and the 'scene' she wanted to present to others. The signs of Chloe's embarrassment impacted further on her 'character' and her image of the 'ideal relationship', influencing the reality of the performance and lifting the presented 'ideal mask' of their relationship, as her friends were given a full glimpse behind the scene of Chloe's performance and their relationship, enabling them to formulate a 'bad impression' of her boyfriend.

When articulating their opinions, the foremost focus was on mutual trust and "no lying – I hate being lied to" (Bonnie), with all the respondents commenting on its importance as the foundation of a healthy relationship. There was also a sense of the need to "feel close and be there for each other" (Chloe) and to be able to rely on each other. This was aligned with the notion of the importance of honesty, being able to "be yourself" (Becky), feel comfortable with each other and have a general feeling of a "strong bond" (Aleysha), loving and being loved. Within the young women's accounts, there was a focus on honesty and communicating effectively, to "tell everything" (Lowri) to your partner and a general need for respect. There was also a sense of the importance of attraction and gaining enjoyment and pleasure from intimate relationships, not only in a physical or sexual manner but also in the feeling of mutual belonging, partnership and the security of "being there for each other" (Chloe). Importance was also placed on being attractive to the opposite sex, in particular, having the perceived attractive body image of what they thought men found attractive in women, for example, "big boobs, shapely bum and a slender waist" (Glesni). Generally, the 'Barbie' description was linked to the perceived ideal physical appearance preferred by young men, reinforcing the stereotype of the representation of the female body as groomed and slim (Smith et al, 1990). The wants and desires as part of sexual attraction and relationship desires were framed in a gendered manner. Young men were again described as hyper-sexual, with their focus on the female body and looks. This was further perpetuated by the notion that young women were judged on their body image, in particular, whether they were fat, which drove their desire to "look better for their boyfriends" (Mali). However, young men were expected to conform to the body image of being strong and masculine – "it's a bit weird if a boy is shorter than me" (Glesni) – and that they should not demonstrate their body insecurities.

On the whole, intimate relationships were seen as challenging, but also with the potential to improve a person due to the apparent requirement to be selfless and prioritise your intimate partner. Within this discussion, the emerging picture was that of young women as selfless and passive. The overall importance was placed on being happy and gaining 'something' positive from a relationship. However, what this 'something' looked like was unclear. Their general beliefs were focused on the importance of being with a partner that added to, rather than deducted from, your life. Despite this, several of the young women's narratives revealed the opposite. Primarily, they drew upon traditional dominant discourses of (hetero)sexuality by positioning themselves as wanting commitment and love from intimate relationships, in particular, the concept of becoming a couple and conforming to relationship expectations focused on romantic ideals, and the need to "feel special" (Collette) and "be together" (Julie). It also became apparent that their agency was limited through the dominance of these normative discourses, and the notion of their role as passive and secondary to their boyfriends'.

Relationship progression and courtship norms

Young intimate relationships differ from adult intimate relationships, specifically, with regard to the role expectations, the degree of intimacy, the duration and everyday routines (Hickman et al, 2004). The majority of first intimate relationships take place during adolescence, with an estimated 88 per cent of young people in some form of intimate partner relationship (Barter et al, 2009), and the likelihood of experiencing abuse within the first relationships higher than subsequent ones (CAADA, 2013). The first sexual experience for young heterosexual women frequently occurs within the context of 'first love relationships' (Hird and Jackson, 2001, p 28). Evidence from the third National Survey of Sexual Attitudes and Lifestyles (Natsal-3) suggests that the percentage of underage sexual experiences has increased for both young men and young women. Furthermore, a significant proportion of young people in the UK report not feeling ready for their first sexual activity, and, as a result, lose their virginity under circumstances that are incompatible with positive sexual health, with just under 40 per cent of women and approximately 26.5 per cent of men sharing a view that their first sexual experience had occurred at the wrong time (Palmer et al, 2019). Young people's intimate relationships are also often the location where gender inequality is perpetuated, due to the limited sexual scripts, gender inequality and the sexist behaviour of young men, which Chung conceptualises as 'masquerading intimacy' (Chung, 2005, p 449).

There was evidence of engagement in established courtship rituals, which appeared reshaped by the ever-dominant presence of social media. Indeed, courtship rituals as a whole appeared to take place on a virtual platform, with the use of Tinder,[1] Facebook, Snapchat and messaging (both instant and text messages) prevalent and taking precedence over face-to-face contact. Establishing a sense of the nature of young intimate relationships was important to me. The first question in the interview schedule focused on how participants defined an intimate relationship, and whether they were 'going out' with anyone at the moment. Despite the consensus that an intimate relationship equated to 'going out', there was no consensus on when a relationship became intimate and when it was 'going out'. Three interesting themes emerged: firstly, the challenge of defining 'going out'; secondly, the use of similar language when defining 'going out'; and, thirdly, the urgency to discuss their intimate relationships with reference to sexual intimacy, rather than in light of the progression of their relationship and the stages of 'going out'. That is, the importance of their intimate relationships was measured with reference to sexual intimacy, which was seen as a key component to the definition of the seriousness of a relationship. There was a general ambiguity as to what actually constituted sexual intimacy, with particular behaviours outside this definition (kissing, touching), while other actions were conceptualised as 'sex' (intercourse). It also appeared that the degree of intimacy, emotions and the regularity of sex factored in whether the sexual intimacy could be defined as part of an intimate relationship.

Intimate relationships were automatically assumed by the participants to be within the framework of heterosexuality. The formation of a 'couple' and a 'relationship' was based on its length, publicity and social identity of both individuals as a 'couple'. Ultimately, the narratives revealed young men as formulating the pace, boundaries and expectations of a relationship. As such, coercion also played a key role, with young women describing circumstances of overt and explicitly sexual coercion. Sexual pressure was expressed as intensifying with age, in particular for young men, with this often excused and nominated as the factor influencing the male sexual priority within intimate relationships. Young men were described as having to "live up" to the expectation that he would want to have sex, to want to have it all the time, with the possibility of leaving school as a virgin ridiculed by their peers:

> 'I know boys who are desperate to lose their virginity … I have a male friend who is desperate to lose his virginity and he has said that he wants to lose it before he leaves school. His friends have slept with more than one girl; society puts more pressure on boys to have sex.' (Grug)

The desperation and pressure to have sex was normalised as the expected masculine role, while this perceived male sexual drive was not seen as having the potential to translate into manipulation, pressure or sexual coercion. The pressure on young men to perform was also visible, as there was a sense of the gendered and heteronormative expectation "you're gay if you don't have an interest in sex" (Chloe).

The 'check and balance' on relationship status and progression was gendered; primarily, young women checked the status, specifically, if the relationship was established and monogamous, as this was a "typical girl thing" (Alyesha). This status check was carefully planned, as "boys feel trapped in relationships as they're laid back … I don't like to nag him [the guy she is meeting up with to have sex] – it's kinda annoying" (Glesni). Additionally, this was packaged in a manner which further drew on traditional gendered discourses by explicitly noting that boys and girls played a different role in intimate relationships, with young men wanting and needing the freedom to go out more. There was a 'mixed' response initially to the planning of activities within relationships, with a few explicit answers that their boyfriends led on the planning front, as "he likes planning, so he decides" (Becky). Becky frames the role of planning their activities within a narrative of choice as individual decisions, rather than a gendered or naturalised issue. This reveals that young men tend to control progression within their intimate relationships, specifically, due to the interpersonal power differences between men and women.

On the surface, it appeared that boys were more 'laid back', and therefore activities were negotiable; when unpicking further, it became apparent that this negotiable space was limited by 'his mood'. Glesni also described that "Sometimes I want more, but he's made it clear that he doesn't want more. He decides what we do". The "more" for Glesni here referred to her wish to have a relationship with an older young man she had been "seeing". Following her separation from her older boyfriend, a few months later, Glesni began seeing her older ex-boyfriend again and described how a pattern had been established that he would ring her when he wanted sex. Her friends were unaware that she had started to "see" this particular young man again, which essentially meant that he would phone her when he wanted to meet up to have sex. She would subsequently see him at parties where he would ignore her and she felt as if she became "invisible". This pattern was accepted, despite her wish to have a stable relationship beyond casual sex, with his behaviour excused by Glesni as "boys find it negative to stick with one girl", and that, stereotypically, "boys are not bothered". There was a general overall sense that "boys were more laid back", with girls seen as the drivers in progressing relations towards an established relationship status. As a result, Glesni accepted the routine of being used for casual sex, despite her wish to rekindle a stable relationship with her ex-boyfriend. This illustrates how young people's choices are limited by their gender and lack of autonomy and power within their intimate relationships.

Delyth described how the progression of her relationship was dictated by her boyfriend, with his request that their relationship remained "secret", as he had previously been in a relationship with her friend. This led to verbal arguments and her reaction needed to be "reserved" to prevent the situation becoming "nasty", but despite her reservation, she would receive a barrage of abusive text messages. This was in direct response to her efforts to establish a public status to their relationship. Delyth described that she was not in a position to challenge his behaviour until he calmed down, often days after the initial argument. Despite this, she justified his actions, as he was being considerate and caring towards her friend's position as his ex-girlfriend, despite her feelings of being placed as "second best". This position was validated when she discovered that he had been seeing his ex-girlfriend, her friend, which ruined their friendship.

Those young women who had no, or limited, experience of intimate relationships reflected on and appeared critical of those who conformed to expected gendered norms. The younger women within the sample who did not have relationship experience appeared more reflective than those within their year group who did in fact have relationship experience. Julie was discouraged from entering an intimate relationship after witnessing her sister's. Her sister, who is older, was in a long-term relationship and had two children. They had moved to another part of the UK and she suffered significant verbal, emotional and physical abuse, resulting in formal court proceedings. Julie described how he would get angry really fast and was frequently angry with them as a family, in particular, when they spoke Welsh. He would refuse to allow her to return home and isolated her from her family and friends. She described how their family had significant concerns about her sister, but continued to be unaware of the full extent of the abuse she suffered, and had felt powerless to intervene. Julie acknowledged the abuse suffered by her sister, and felt that witnessing the impact of this abuse on her sister and her family as a whole has made her wary of having an intimate relationship in the future. As such, she described her limited relationship experience, and reiterates Glesni's view that "Boys find it negative to stick with one girl".

Mostly, the young women indicated that the progression of their relationship was largely controlled by their boyfriends. This behaviour was located within a framework of justification and naturalisation of the male role, rather than as controlling behaviour. Young women did not express any desire to take more of an active role in determining the progress of their intimate relationships. This was because seeming to be keen could have negative implications, such as rejection: "they won't want you" (Alyesha) or "being used for sex" (Michelle). Young men's desire for an exclusive relationship, or any degree of commitment, was seen as ambivalent, to say the least. When a degree of commitment was offered, this often crossed the boundary to become controlling and oppressive. There were examples of more balanced relationships: "we spend time together, but it tends to be around friends and our sporty stuff" (Claire). The pace of progression appeared to be linked to the desire and ability of young men to have sex with their girlfriends/prospective girlfriends. This often resulted in shame, disappointment and potentially significant consequences for the young women. There was a general essentialist belief that young men naturally take the lead regarding particular relationship developments, so that they can 'do gender' and perform their masculine role. There were also evident social sanctions for non-conformation with the expected gendered scripts, such as the process of 'unfriending' or being 'uninvited' from social events. Most of the peer discussion surrounded young men, relationships and sex, and those not engaging in this behaviour were excluded. As Claire describes: "You want to be part of the conversation; you don't have anything to talk about if you haven't had sex. We are a group of 12 friends; ten of the 12 have had sex and half of our group are in a relationship". The direct consequence of non-conforming was also linked to control, rejection and the feeling of 'being left on the shelf'. There was evidence across the interviews of a degree of discussion and negotiation around the timing of first sexual contact. In all cases, discussions on this first contact were initiated by boyfriends, with their timetables and outcomes prioritised.

Gender norms and relationship roles

Participants reflected a belief that they should feel 'lucky' to be in an intimate relationship, with a sense of loss and embarrassment if this aim had not been achieved. There was a general sense of 'success' when a young woman was 'selected' to undertake the 'girlfriend role' and should therefore settle for a boy willing to be part of a relationship. This reinforced the belief that young women valued relationships more than young men, as it is the role of young men to do the asking and for the young women to accept their offer. It can be argued that such a sense of gratefulness, as well as the impression of a relationship, in defining success can result in young women remaining in unhealthy relationships. In comparison, young men were described as having a sense of entitlement which placed them in a position of power, as the young women generally felt fortunate when they committed to an intimate relationship. This perceived 'luck' was expanded further when there was a sense that their social position within their peer group was improved, resulting in party invitations and inclusion in the conversations about sex and relationships. The absence of an intimate relationship was conceptualised as a void, which resulted in a natural exclusion from the conversation (Claire) and had a knock-on effect on their popularity and visibility (Becky). This was also seen as a measure of individual maturity and preparation for adulthood. Conversely, this increased participation often came at a price, as several narratives illustrated that increased attendance at parties or social events often led to arguments, jealousy and close surveillance by their boyfriends. The pressure to gain relationship experience and avoid exclusion from peer conversations was unavoidable, due to its overwhelming presence in all forms of online and offline spaces. This was in sharp contrast to the automatic entitlement of young men to attend parties and social gatherings, and maintain a much more explicit online presence on social media sites (discussed in further detail in the next chapter).

Boyfriends often questioned why their girlfriends wanted or needed to spend time with their friends, as it was perceived that it should be enough that they now had a boyfriend, which they saw as a full-time emotional commitment. The young women themselves would limit the time they spent with their friends once they entered a relationship. However, there were dissenting voices illustrating the belief that young women should not be "too clingy" (Donna) within a mature relationship, as it is important to allocate time for friends and family, not just boyfriends. The agenda was often set by their boyfriends, with the implications of going against this routine often resulting in arguments, verbal abuse, increased controlling behaviour and the general sense that he was 'in a mood', which was mentioned by several young women (Michelle, Elen, Lowri, Rhiannon). When young men got 'in a mood', the young women became compliant by modifying their behaviour in response to the increased demands of their boyfriends. The young women described how they constantly had to negotiate their behaviour and social space, both online and offline.

When the young women became jealous, rather than becoming controlling, they would often respond by providing a greater degree of freedom and would make additional allowances; for example, they would consciously not ask their boyfriends about pictures posted on Facebook of them with another young woman. This general response to be passive and less questioning was due to the anxiety of "not being wanted" (Alyesha). The young women demonstrated a fear of being 'dropped' if they acted upon their jealousy and insecurities. Again, this demonstrates Goffman's 'impression management' and the emotion work of staging their performance to maintain their position as the 'ideal' girlfriend rather than demonstrate the insecurity of a 'nagging' girlfriend. Participants ridiculed their gendered position in order to justify inappropriate male behaviour by describing normative female traits as "girls can get crazy and weird" (Becky) or going "into psycho girlfriend mode" (Aleysha). These references were in relation to the acceptability of male jealousy, which was described as a positive trait, illustrating care, attention and the perceived male competitive streak. Female jealousy was described as unattractive and unjustified, while male requests around time management, "dropping" your friends and shaping your life around their needs was justified and mostly accepted; for example:

'They tend to not fit in [friends]. Like, I feel really bad because I'm always making excuses, like, I can't see you, but I think, with uni coming up, we're going to be drifting apart anyway, so I think this is the process for me to be drifting apart from them, kind of thing. Like, I always ... I know it's quite mean, but I always make excuses. Like, I would actually rather just be with him than be with my friends because I tend to ... because I think it's a lot more effort being with my friends at the moment, because they're quite hyperactive and things, but it is nice just to have a chilled night in, kind of thing, so I do tend to not sort of fit them in.' (Becky)

Their explanation of jealous behaviour was gender-specific and naturalised, with young men constructed as competitive and protective, while describing their own emotions as irrational.

Across the narratives, there was a general lack of reflection on the discrepancy between the young women's perception of a healthy relationship and their actual relationship experiences. This was illustrated by the efforts that went into the management of their emotions, which was normalised, specifically, how they were required to hide their real emotions in order to avoid rejection, again reflecting complex emotion work. The relationship roles conceptualised by the young women utilised traditional binaries of women as caring and emotional, while men were seen as stable and cool. The young women implicitly subscribed to this categorisation and drew upon biological gender narratives; for example, "Girls are more open and emotional. ... Boys are less emotional; they tend to keep it together a bit more" (Becky). Here, 'emotions' equate to rationality and young men's perceived ability to "keep it together" as they removed emotions from their prescribed role, while young women were "open" and therefore "emotional". Indeed, young women were described as "caring" and "emotional", while, in contrast, young men were described as dominant and quick to "get in a mood". The common excuse offered for their partners' limited emotional response was due to "boys being boys" (Bonnie), and the general concern for the young men's emotion. For example, Michelle's view was that "his mood" was "fair enough" as he had waited to have sex with her, reflecting a view that young men are more typically aligned with the notion of a dating script focused on achieving sexual aspirations. It was expected that young women had to do the work to sustain a close relationship.

Emotion work was also visible within young women's management and negotiation of their own emotions and those of young men. That is, they would lower their expectations, rather than challenge behaviour contrary to their ideal perception of a healthy relationship. Therefore, they did not reduce their expectations because they felt that their ideal image was misguided, but rather to avoid rejection and due to the fear of "not being wanted" (Alyesha). This suggested that young women regarded their intimate relationship opportunities as limited and not to be wasted. These adopted reactive relationship scripts reflect that young men receive greater benefits from young intimate relationships, as young women manage their own emotions to respond to their relationship in a socially desirable manner.

Several participants described the 'open' and 'trusting' nature of young women, in particular, their need to discuss their feelings, problems and relationship quandaries, reflecting their attribution of their behaviour to innate biology. There was also a sense that young women lose their inhibitions and talk more openly about their emotions in particular circumstances: "We [girls] mostly talk about our feelings when we are drunk and we push the confidence level", while "Boys are less emotional – tend to keep it together a bit more" (Becky). This stereotype of how young men and young women feel, and, ultimately, how 'emotional' they act, was identified as a factor influencing their gender performance. It appeared that framing their intimate relationships within these traditional scripts reaffirmed their expectations, essentially providing a degree of stability. The perception of the 'openness' of young women and the restraint of "keep[ing] it together" of young men was generally seen as complementary within a relationship. The implications are that these forms of hegemonic expectations reproduce the acceptable level of emotion that can be expressed by both genders. Some of the young women drew upon internalised gendered stereotypes, in order to reproduce, rather than challenge, damaging norms that often underpinned abusive behaviour within their intimate relationships. The implication of these statements is that participants referred to essentialist notions of young men's natural desire to be dominant, controlling and sexual. The focus was on sexual conquests, with the aim of boasting and "be[ing] big-headed about things they had done [sexual]" and describing "I did this and that with her" (Lowri). This boasting trait again was naturalised as a male desire, with young women described as "not want[ing] to say" (Lowri) and being more private about their sexual relationships and desires. The young women reported different gendered patterns of talking about intimacy, with young men perceived as talking openly about sex, while young women talked about their desires to be wanted. Even within long-term relationships, it was implied that the boundary around secrecy and privacy changed with time: "After a while, he didn't seem to care who he told [that they had sex]. He told his friends" (Chloe).

The young women within this research wanted a relationship with older boys, at least two years older, with young men noted, in contrast, as preferring girls younger than themselves. Their preferences mirror the patterns of young intimate relationships documented in Barter et al (2009). Several participants described the ideal relationship as the image exemplified by romantic films:

> 'Girls are more focused on romantic films and lots of films say that this is the expectations and this is what happens in society. Boys don't really watch films – they don't like them – they like stuff more like video games and things that aren't true, while girls get a fixed view on what's okay and expected in relationships.' (Chloe)

While the depictions within video games were seen as unrealistic, in contrast, the ideals within romantic films were normalised and related more to reality. Chloe articulates a key difference between films and video games, that girls are more aligned with the reality of relationships and learn the expected norms from romantic films. She describes that girls get a "fixed view" of what's deemed as "OK" in relationships from the "romance" of films, which she felt was the "truth" of relationship expectations. There was a general sense that being 'soppy' was good, but that this was a female attribute:

> 'Just tell me how he feels, which is nice, because guys don't normally like to do that a lot but, yeah, he likes telling me what he's feeling. And I'm not as soppy as he is. So it's sort of like, normally the girl is quite soppy, but I'm not as soppy, but I will … when I'm feeling like it, I'll share.' (Becky)

Becky described how her boyfriend's behaviour is different, "which is nice", and demonstrates how he is prepared to share his emotions and relinquish a degree of his power as part of this role reversal. Even though Becky's relationship did not follow the 'emotional' expectations she describes, she does not question this norm; rather, she draws on essential beliefs that "normally the girl is quite soppy" to reinforce this norm. She described how, within their relationship, their gendered roles are performed, specifically, the need for women to be the caregiver and males to be the provider. Becky positions the adoption of a masculine role in a complementary manner, or as a foil to her perceived need of women to "look after" or care for "guys".

The idea of 'love', pleasure and desire

Love was seen as an important aspect of young people's intimate relationships, and was generally viewed as part of a romantic relationship rather than linked to infatuation, passion or commitment. When discussing their wishes for their relationships, love and their desire to be loved featured heavily as part of the young women's narratives. Collette explained that her ideal person would be "somebody that makes me feel loved, cares for me and makes me feel special", with Becky stating that she felt that "honesty and love" were required together as, within a relationship, you needed to "actually love someone". The feeling of being loved in a relationship was associated with happiness, feeling good, being cared for and 'belonging'.

Some of the young women held idealistic notions of 'love'. For example, Bella explained that when she first met a boy she had been talking to via social media, they hugged and they both then said that they "loved" each other. She explained that they repeated this when they met on the second occasion and that her boyfriend initiated the "hug", which she felt was "cute". Glain explained that some of her friends in school just want a boyfriend/girlfriend and, as a result, do not think about "true love", as they think about being in a relationship as a popularity thing. Jennifer explained that while her boyfriend said "I love you", he didn't generally show affection:

Interviewer: How does he show affection, then?

Jennifer: He's not really like that; he doesn't really show how … he's not really a loving person, really. He says he loves you and stuff, but he doesn't really show it; he's not a very clingy person.

The notion of 'love' was also linked to the progression of relationships, and was associated with exclusivity and a long-term, committed relationship. There was also a sense that saying "I love you" is important and should not be used flippantly:

Interviewer: What do you think is the key thing that makes the 'kind of' seeing someone to a relationship difference? What's the key difference between both?

Aleysha: It's when they say, "I love you". I think that's a big thing. I think it's overused these days. Like, people say, "oh, I love you", "I love you too", but I think your feelings mean something.

Interviewer: So if you guys were to tell each other in the next few weeks now, that you loved each other, would that then promote it to the status of a relationship?

Aleysha: I don't know. I think it's all really early stages. We've not got … we do know each other, but we don't know each other as much as I want to.

Interviewer: So it's time, as well.

Bonnie described how she had embraced her boyfriend's life, had fallen in love with him, his daughter and his dog:

Interviewer: So if he does show affection at any time, would it be cuddling or kissing or …?

Bonnie: Yeah. No one else has ever meant that much to me, either. And I've never fallen in love with somebody's dog before. And do you know what, after him, as well; I'm not going for a boy with a dog. I'm not doing that again. No.

Bonnie goes on to explain how she felt when she argued with her boyfriend and they separated for a couple of weeks and how much she missed his dog!

'Horrible. It was really horrible, OK? Because then he was like, oh, yeah, you can still see the dog and that, OK, and my mate, he was watching so I went there to see the dog, yeah, and then, OK, he turns up on the cob and I was like, oh my God, what are you doing here? I'm like pissed off with him, like, why have you turned up here? And he was looking proper cute in his jeans that I love him wearing and everything, and it was like, oh, this is horrible, yeah. The boy I love standing, like, right there. And I was like, I can't do anything. It's like ahhh. It's OK. It's all good now.' (Bonnie)

The idea of love was also brought up when some of the young women were discussing prevention education. Bonnie explains what she would advise those young women who are in an unhealthy relationship, but believe that they love their boyfriend:

'I don't know, I'd just talk to the kids and that, yeah. And then just basically tell them what's not right and what's not normal and that. Just like, if this ever happens, the signs of stuff, and if them signs are there you've just got to … it doesn't matter how much you think you love him, just got to kick him, or you're just going to stay with him and it's going to be really, really, really bad and you're just going to be like …' (Bonnie)

The importance of leaving an unhealthy relationship was highlighted, irrespective of any feelings of love; however, this did not necessarily translate into practice when participants described their intimate relationship experiences, as illustrated in earlier themes of this chapter.

Reflections: the power of gendered norms

The attitudes voiced by the young women failed to translate into their own intimate relationships. What was evident instead was a tendency to naturalise and justify sexist and abusive behaviours. What this illustrates is the trend for young women to become the 'passive' or 'reactive' girlfriend, in particular, when faced with harassment, controlling behaviour and unwanted attention. The presence of gendered norms was damaging for young women in three distinct ways. Firstly, due to the construction of the young women's propensity to be 'emotional'; secondly, due to their perceived sexual weakness in contrast to male dominance and desire; and, thirdly, because of the justification and naturalisation of emotional, abusive and coercive behaviour. If we are to understand the nature and patterns of abuse in teenage relationships, then we must acknowledge how young people construct meanings about their sexual selves, their relationship aspirations, their understanding and their attitudes towards 'good' and 'bad' relationships. The gaps between young women's expectations and lived experiences were clear. Their attitudes were focused on an ideology of equality, whereas their intimate relationship experiences generally revealed their limited and unequal power base. This indicates the challenges posed by a post-feminist discourse, where narratives and expectations about equalisation and aspirations are far removed from their real positions in intimate relationships. This discourse of equality instead served to minimise the visibility of the abuse for some of the young women, who utilised the language of choice and biologically driven narratives in order to explain and justify existing relationship inequalities. However, some of them were also able to recognise unequal positions, mostly after the end of relationships.

There was a general resistance towards, as well as a justification of, somewhat subtle forms of coercion, harassment and control. The extent of acceptability was shaped by their image of traditional gendered norms and expectations. In many instances, the young women failed to propose an alternative script to the hegemonic masculinity they were experiencing within their own intimate relationships. The popular narratives of men's 'nature' – "that's how they are" and "I'm just a 'psycho bitch'" (Aleysha) – were reinforced when prioritising what young men wanted from relationships, primarily, as a result of the fear of rejection. Not only did this reinforce the perspective that male demands and desires were prioritised but also that the notion of casual sex was accepted, as men were constructed as naturally commitment-phobic. This sense of symbolic gendering revealed the perceived benefits and comfort gained from accepting established gendered scripts, rather than suffering the consequences of non-conformity. Thus, it was permitted and expected for young men to have a focus on the physicality of intimate relationships. The ingrained fear of transgressing gender norms and challenging this sexual emphasis placed young women within the quandary of 'sexual double standards'. It was apparent that they lacked the power to operationalise their egalitarian attitudes in order to engage in relationships that adhere to the description of what they expect, want or desire within a 'healthy relationship'. As a default position, they relied and drew upon normative scripts focused on essentialist beliefs. Therefore, their claim of gender equality does not translate into their everyday relationships, further concealing and reinforcing their lack of power, negotiation and choice.

The young women's narratives illustrated the task of challenging young men's power due to the cultural attitudes that perpetuate established, static, gendered identities, which favour men over women; preparing young men to relinquish their power needs to be incorporated as part of prevention education. Furthermore, when re-evaluating the balance of power between young women and young men, young women's confidence and agency requires further consideration. This re-evaluation will assist these women to construct their position in a manner that reduces the likelihood that any form of negotiation and power comes at a cost. This cost was seen within their narratives as the emotion work of the management of this power imbalance, due to the lack of negotiating space within their intimate relationships. Key messages for future research are also identified: primarily, the need to focus on healthy relationship education and gendered norms. The discussion here suggests that this needs to include a focus on sexual identities, consent, privacy and the use of social media. There is a sense that the behaviour of boyfriends was seen as their entitlement due to their power, while young women attempted to make themselves 'invisible' to avoid judgement, comments or being ostracised. As a result, within the current context, young women's scope and power to reshape established gendered scripts of relationships and femininities is limited.

4

The gendered 'doing of sex': sexual double standards

The dichotomy of a slag/angel and gendered 'sexual double standards' is a challenging dilemma for young women from the standpoint of their attitudinal understanding and experiences. These women face the everyday complexity of the deconstruction of female sexuality, specifically, the contradictory constructions of femininity that promote sexual allure, while also asserting control over female sexuality. The 'doing of sex' for young women ignites a web of controversy and dilemma, often placing them in an impossible position. Young women demonstrate both a challenging and condoning attitude towards the double morality of the differential labelling of young women's and men's expected sexual behaviours.

The practice of slut shaming (Ringrose and Renold, 2012) and the derogatory labelling of young women stigmatise them, while labels on young men as 'lads' promote their sexual agency (Fjaer et al, 2015). Social norms of gender and the image of a slut limit the role of young women to be 'passive', in particular, around their sexual identity and desires. The challenge faced by these women is of negotiating a female identity, with shifting appropriateness dictated by the requirement to be virginal, while also being available to sexually please the opposite sex. Continuously, young women are subjected to a 'double standard', whereby sexually active young men are labelled as the 'norm', and sexually active young women are stigmatised. As stated by Hird and Jackson, 'Young women, as "gate-keepers" of heterosexual relations, must negotiate complex and contradictory discourses that penalise membership in both "sluts" and "angel" categories' (2001, p 35). Young women are placed on a tightrope in order to negotiate this binary of the angel/slut, which can often impact on their identity and emotional well-being.

The young women interviewed revealed the constant pressure on them to perform the overt sexual role, often being judged as a 'slag/slut' by their peers and the wider community. However, despite acknowledgement by young women that this is problematic and an unfair label, this is also perpetuated by these women themselves. Pervasive 'double standards' exist in relation to girls' and boys' sexual activity, which function as a dichotomy for young women of angelic femininity and the stigmatised sexual slut/slag/whore, illustrating the precarious nature of their sexual reputation, in sharp contrast to young men's laddish/sexual hero role. Heteronormative assumptions function as a barrier to reshaping sexualised roles of young women and, indeed, young men. These assumptions reinforce these gendered requirements, which are also reflected in the media, specifically, the images perpetuated by popular youth cultures and the porn industry. There is also a challenge for young men to adhere to normative standards of the hegemonic male, with the provision of limited space for them to negotiate their identities beyond this static hegemonic script. Young women's identities often became 'spoilt' when they act in a manner that is perceived to be contrary to social norms and the presumed 'natural' sexual passivity expected of them.

The discussion ahead will focus on the challenges faced by the young women of negotiating intersecting female identities, with shifting appropriateness of this 'double standard' dictated by the requirement to be virginal, while also being available to sexually please young men. Young women are constantly on the negative receiving end of 'sexual double standards', where all options available within their power leave them open to the judgement of others. Young men are perceived to have the social permission to focus on the sexual physicality of intimate relationships, while young women experience the ingrained fear of transgressing gender norms and challenging this sexual emphasis, thus placing them within the quandary of 'sexual double standards'.

Schooling sexual identities

The literature on young people and masculinity highlights the role and influence of education and schooling environments as agents of socialisation, which is germane to the discussion here. Schools are sites for 'compulsory heterosexuality' (Nayak and Kehily, 2008), reinforcing institutional regimes of power and gender. The gendered nature of sexualisation within schools happens much earlier within a framework of gendered playground games. The normalisation of 'everyday' sexual harassment on the basis that 'boys will be boys' is (re)asserted within the power of male patriarchal dominance (Renold, 2013). The objectification of girls and young women by young men, and young women's experience of sexual harassment and assault in schools, is also of concern. Sexual harassment functions as a precursor to the acceptability and perpetration of violence and abuse (Stein and Gadin, 2017), and is linked to sexual homophobic bullying in schools (Rivers and Duncan, 2013) and to the display of sexual harmful behaviour (Smith et al, 2013).

Schools conform to established and reinforced gender stereotypes, through sexist attitudes and traditional curriculum content. The young women described negotiating their identity and well-being within educational settings, which actively restricted their identity, behaviour, physical choices and liberty. For example, one school promoted the use of separate gyms, segregated by gender, and gym lessons for boys and girls, which went to the extent of essentially excluding all young women from cross-country as they would not want to take part, or "ruin their hair". Not only does this assume that the primary focus for young women is their appearance, it also labels them as one generic group. The concept of 'schooling sexualities' (Epstein and Johnson, 1998) is central here, as schools are sexualised spaces where identities are (re)produced (Nayak and Kehily, 2008) and typically driven by heteronormative and peer socialisation, negotiated through various cultural, educational and leisure forums.

The young women's narratives revealed a pattern of disparaging remarks and harassment which further served to control their behaviour, along with the message that 'subtly' performing their feminine role was the solution to avoiding judgement and abuse, as "image and peer pressure is a chain" (Glain). For example, Glain described the harassment experienced by her and her friends, including catcalling and daily insults: "If you're thin you're OK; if you're not, they call you a pig". Insults were focused on appearance, in particular, body image, dress choice and make-up. The wearing of certain make-up was seen as overt sexual behaviour, outside the boundaries of what was judged as decent femininity. Glain and Grug described the norm of teachers monitoring make-up and attending classrooms with a wet wipe to remove make-up judged as outside the school or accepted social standards. Their physicality was associated with sexuality, with dress standards and make-up monitored, ensuring that young women remained 'subtle' and that any effort to appear attractive or overtly sexual remained 'invisible'. This requirement of subtlety transferred to their narratives of how their appearance and behaviours required restraint in order to avoid overtly presenting their sexuality, which may cause shock, offence or perceived sexual availability. As a result, throughout the interview, Glain reiterated how she managed her behaviour and appearance to maintain her respect: "I have respect because I haven't done anything". Glain restricted her behaviour and felt fearful of engaging in any form of sexual contact outside the remit of a well-established and long-standing intimate relationship. Basically, she wanted to explicitly demonstrate her role as a 'good girl', and placed limits on her behaviour and was comfortable being 'subtle' and conforming to traditional scripts. Glain adopted her own strategy to regulate her behaviour in order to ensure passivity and inhibit asserting herself sexually, which denied her sexual agency.

Slags and angels: the 'doing of sex'

As mentioned, the deconstruction of female sexuality is complex, due to contradictory constructions of femininity that promote sexual allure, while also asserting control over female sexuality. The dichotomy of a slag/angel and the gendered 'sexual double standards' was a challenging dilemma for participants from their attitudinal understanding and experiences. Overt sexual behaviour for the young women was aligned with being a 'slag/

slut' and, despite the acknowledgement that this was problematic and an unfair label, it remained mostly unchallenged and perpetuated by the young women themselves. In comparison to the attitudes on gendered norms, the response to this issue of 'sexual double standards' was mixed. The percentage of responses that disagreed with this category of questions was lower, with the exception of the response to the statement asking if 'it's OK for boys to "sleep around"', as over 90 per cent disagreed that this was acceptable. While their judgement on whether or not they expected a boyfriend to be faithful was clear, their reaction to whether 'girls who "sleep around" are "slags"' was unclear. From those who responded outside the 'I don't know' category, their responses were evenly separated between those who agreed and those who disagreed with this notion of a 'slag'.

This struggle with the concept of a 'slag', and indeed 'sluts', was further explored in the interviews. The 'doing of sex' for the young women ignited a web of controversy and dilemma, often placing them in an impossible position. Despite this notion of a 'slag' as the overtly sexualised woman, 65 per cent of participants disagreed that young men should be the main instigators of sexual activity. However, 25 per cent agreed that young women should not instigate sexual activity and that therefore it should be young men who are focused on being 'up for sex'. This raised an interesting question around gendered social norms, and when the label of 'slut/slag' is applied and whether sexually active behaviour outside the relationship arena is conceptualised differently. Glesni describes that, "Boys and girls play a different role in relationships cos boys want to go out more and they feel trapped in relationships". Across the young women's narratives, there was a general reinforcement of the male sexual drive discourse, that men have an inherent and natural sex drive, while they generally described themselves as passive and lacking desire. While the young women wanted a relationship, the relationships described functioned as a 'means to an end' for the young men, specifically, their desire to have sex. Ceri describes her view that boys have "more pressure to 'do things' [have sex] rather than being in a relationship. The sexual experience is more important for boys" (Ceri). When the advances of a boyfriend are openly rejected and he has to follow her, the judgement continues to fall on the girlfriend, as illustrated:

'One boy acts like a chauffeur and follows her [his girlfriend] around. She treats him badly when he tries to show affection, she physically pushes him away when he tries to put his hands round her waist. He is like a dog following her. When they separated after a week, she was talking to someone else.' (Glain)

Glain judges this young woman for demonstrating assertive behaviour and emotional distance within her relationship.

Young women's sexual role is limited by the ingrained notion of them as sexual beings synonymous with being a slut/slag/whore, as Glain described:

Interviewer:	So if a girl has a boyfriend, she's called a slut?
Glain:	Yes, and when she doesn't have one. I was walking with my friends and then she said, "look at these big sluts".
Interviewer:	When you were walking on the street?
Glain:	When they are alone, it's OK; when boys are in a big group, they call us slut.
Interviewer:	When does it happen?
Glain:	Every Friday cos there lots on the street – they'll say, look at the little slut, the minger. I just think, OK, if that's what you want to say!
Interviewer:	Will they say anything about the body?
Glain:	Yes, but people think I'm thin, so I'm OK. People don't really say anything about me cos they have respect for me – yes! Well, hopefully!
Interviewer:	Why do you think you have this respect?
Glain:	Cos I haven't done anything not to have it. I'm never out, well I am, but I don't drink. I have a job; I work hard and I'm nice with everyone. There's lots of people they hate each other. I hate some people but I'm still nice to them.
Interviewer:	So you think that's important to get respect. Who are these boys?
Glain:	They are about year or two less than me; they say sluts, minger and other words just out of the blue.

This example demonstrates that sexual harassment is driven by cultural stereotypes about gender and sexuality that reinforce imbalanced power relationships. For the young women, name calling was also a norm within their intimate relationships:

'My friends didn't like him cos he would call me names like "slag". He would call me a "slag" and I would swear at him. The arguments would start when he would come up to me and accuse me of things, but I would argue back. He would try to show that I was the "bad one" – "why have you said that we have done this and that?" or "why are you meeting with the lads?"' (Lowri)

This verbal abuse was naturalised as part of the jealous male role, was often played out within public spaces, primarily the school, and often attempted to discredit the perceived actions of their girlfriends.

The available gendered script is static and places expectations on young people to conform to particular unrealistic sexual ideals. The pressures of conforming to masculine expectations was acknowledged and often illustrated to justify their boyfriends' behaviours: "They want to show they're cool, and don't want to be left out with their mates" (Lowri). Young men were described as purely having a sexual motive, and wanting to know if young women "are good in bed" or "if you will do certain things [sexual]" (Glain), and the general expectation that "women need to do more sexually [sex acts]" (Jennifer). In Jennifer's case, she had been with her boyfriend for over a year and explained that their relationship had become acrimonious, describing that there was "quite a lot of arguing ... everything builds up ... if he's in a mood". She described that a key trigger for their arguments was his open discussion with his friends about their sex life, the influence of porn on their relationship and, in particular, his request to have a threesome, which made her feel that "basically, I've got to do what makes him happy". This all demonstrated his power to degrade and humiliate her, but also illustrated her growing understanding of this unhealthy practice and her growing willingness to challenge his behaviour.

Jennifer described that her boyfriend "sees how girls are in these films [porn films] and is influenced by it. They get paid, I'm not and I'm not doing everything. Boys naturally want threesomes – why?" Jennifer explained the pressure she felt to please her boyfriend by doing "more sexually", which he then discussed in the school common room with his friends. Her boyfriend's wish to have a threesome is naturalised and excused as part of his biological sexual desire. The emotion work for Jennifer was apparent, specifically, how she attempted to hide her disgust and indeed her choice not to have a threesome with her boyfriend. She felt trapped by her limited negotiation space and the apparent demand to prioritise her boyfriend's desires, which he openly discussed with their peers. Her initial unwanted feelings of disgust had been 'managed' and suppressed during the course of this relationship. However, she was now revealing her wish to end this relationship and therefore felt more able to evoke her true feelings, which had increased her arguments with her boyfriend. Despite this increase, Jennifer was continuing to challenge her boyfriend's demands and was working to prioritise her desires. By doing so, she also could not envisage a future for this relationship. Jennifer, on the one hand, describes how she maintains her girlfriend role within the 'open' common room chat about her sex life, while on a private level, she has begun to challenge her boyfriend's lack of respect for her privacy. Goffman's (1963) concept of the performance of the self, specifically how characters play a role to satisfy the audience, assists in understanding Jennifer's performance and demonstration of her relationships in front of their peers, despite the fact that she could voice her concerns and feelings with a close friend, and during the research interview, she lacked the space and power to challenge his behaviour in front of their peers. For the time being, she is maintaining her 'facework' (Goffman, 1955).

Jennifer distanced herself from the women portrayed in these films "as they get paid", while naturalising his apparent sexual desire to have a threesome. She also separates herself from sex workers who are paid to feign desire and sexual pleasure to conform to male expectations. She expressed her concerns regarding the influence of pornography on her boyfriend's expectations; implicit in this is the recognition of porn as a tool to satisfy male needs and the submission of women. She linked her boyfriend's consumption of porn to her belief that boys/young men want threesomes, or sex with multiple partners at the same time. She was concerned about the influence of porn on her boyfriend and their relationship status, in particular, the portrayal of women and the connotations of this objectification on his expectations of her, due to this depiction of sex. Jennifer reflected that she felt the influence of porn was shameful and degrading, basically emulating acts that she would not want to do. This aligns with research that more young men than young women want to intentionally access and emulate pornography (Martellozzo et al, 2016), as they feel less shame towards it and do not acknowledge that it is degrading to women (Johansson and Hammaren, 2007).

The precarious nature of young women's sexual reputation was in sharp contrast to young men's laddish/sexual hero role. Claire described that:

> 'It's easier for boys to sleep around. They get called a "lad", girls get called "sluts". Girls get a "bad name" – slag. But she's not like that [her friend] – she was really into this guy – she was called a slag by the boys in our year and in the year above [after Claire's friend had slept with her boyfriend].' (Claire)

There was also a general distaste if young men went to extremes and demonstrated overt "vulgar" or sexual behaviour. Elen explained that her boyfriend's "vulgar behaviour" translated into his routine reference of her as a "slag or harlot", which would be on a daily basis, in particular, when they argued or he became jealous. She used language (vulgar) that minimised his behaviour of using words to verbally abuse, degrade and humiliate her, which she did not recognise as abusive behaviour, despite the fact that she was reflecting on their relationship which had ended due to his abusive behaviour.

Young women portray themselves in a sexualised manner on social media, which often results in negative consequences. A year 9 pupil in one school sent a video clip of herself masturbating via Facebook to another pupil; she had not intended that this video would then be shared with her peers and across her local community. As this video was sent via Facebook rather than Snapchat, the clip was saved and subsequently circulated to the whole school community without her consent. As a result, she was labelled a 'slag' in the school, and indeed across the community. She was ostracised and described as now "having no one". Only one research participant empathised with her position by realising that this had "affected her", as "the girls in year 10 are like cats ... they won't let it go – they are worse than the boys" (Mair). Therefore, she was judged harshly by the majority of her female peers for acting contrary to the expected norms, and expressing her female desires. The version(s) of this story shaped the moral and sexual landscape of the school for the pupils, moulding all social aspects of student conversations. This was explicitly exposed when she was the only young woman in her year group not to participate in the questionnaire stage of this research. Interestingly, these observations were also shared by participants who did not have any previous or current intimate relationship experience:

> 'A year 9 girl sent a video of herself via Facebook, someone saved it and then circulated the video – she was masturbating in the video. She was called a "slut", she was upset, but also bragging about it. ... No one cares if a boy does that [masturbating] cos a video of a boy masturbating was also sent round the school. He didn't come to school for a week and then it was forgotten, but with this girl, it went on for a long time.' (Julie)

Alexis described another event:

> 'There have been a couple of incidents in the school regarding inappropriate photos. There was a year 9 incident and a big argument in the hallway. A girl from year 9 had photos of a year 11 girl on her phone. People shouted and had a go at the year 9 girl. The teachers didn't interfere for quite a long time. The girls were called slags. It wouldn't have lasted for such a long time if it was a boy, in particular, a well respected boy.' (Alexis)

And there was yet another version by Mair: "A year 10 girl shared photos with everyone – everyone turned against her and called her a slag. She has no one; she sits on her own. She does with people, but they aren't real with her. I would say that this has affected her. Everything's forgotten with boys".

There was a sense of panic around this young woman's overt sexual action, resulting in her stigmatisation by her peers and the wider community. Indeed, the moral debate and the panic had arisen from the knowledge that she masturbated and dared to explore sexual pleasure. Conversely, similar behaviour by a young man was described as "ancient history" and he was then a "bit of a legend". The labels of 'slag', 'slut' or 'whore' were endured as a form of misery by this young woman and exercised through the social mechanisms of reputation. She was still unable to redeem herself months after the incident; indeed, it was still a 'hot topic' at the end of my fieldwork, nearly a year after the incident. This young woman was subjected to these labels as a symbol of shame, with this prolonged by rumours, bravados and mythical stories of overt female sexuality, and with the sharing of this rumour used as a form of social currency (Marwick and Boyd, 2014) in order to build the recognition of some at her expense due to her 'spoiled identity' (Goffman, 1963) and behaviour contrary to social norms and presumed 'natural' sexual passivity in women. As a result of how she was seen and located by 'others' (as an outsider), she was ostracised, not only by her peers but also by the wider community. This illustrates how shame and embarrassment promote self-control through a social hierarchy focused on rewarding those who align their behaviour with gendered social norms.

This young woman's behaviour and identity attracted moral opposition, as it was contrary to the ritual order of social interaction (Goffman, 1959). Managing this stigmatisation required emotion work. This story symbolised the young woman as a shameful figure, to be ridiculed and avoided, with the similar incident of the young man used as a foil to illustrate her desperate position. The young man's sexual exploits were accepted as a 'joke' and a positive demonstration of his sexuality. While his actions were naturalised ("boys will be boys"), hers were seen as shameful. The power of these rumours and insults increased as the social consequences of such labelling became apparent, highlighting the risk for young women when demonstrating their sexual desires. I would argue that her shaming was a reaction to her demonstration of sexual power, rather than the sexual act itself, and the subsequent attempts of her peers to control her power to limit her 'doing' of gender (West and Zimmerman, 1987). The teachers played a distant or invisible role in both stories, despite their visibility in the formation of the school's sexual culture. This example provides insight into rumour spreading as a form of sexualised bullying, the gatekeeping of gender norms and how they contribute to the constructions of femininity and sexuality when young women demonstrate what is perceived as unacceptable sexual behaviour.

Gender differences are partly attributed to the persistence of a gendered double standard in dominant discourses of social media and young relationships. For example, it is young women who continue to be shamed and judged for engaging in sexting practices in circumstances where sexting is misused or misjudged. The role of gossip functioned as a tool for controlling behaviour and providing these young women with negative feedback on her behaviour. As this example illustrates, the violation of established gendered norms of sexuality resulted in social control through punishment, in the form of isolation and bullying. There is a continued pressure on young women to be sexually active in order to please young men, and only within particular scenarios: either the 'slut' of the threesome or as part of a long-term intimate relationship, with the 'slag' label 'stamped on' for several reasons. Even this latter scenario was often questioned: "Girls call other girls "slags" as well just because she's slept with someone, when's she's not a slag, even if she's in a relationship" (Grug). However, young women also monitor the behaviour of their peers in order to to reinforce their own status, as Mair described how she was often the unwilling bystander to rumour spreading, as the girls are "much worse than the boys". Mair felt that this "watchful eye" is used to form the distinction between those who are subtle/get it right and those who are sexual/get it wrong. Young women who were 'up for sex' were branded with a myriad of derogatory labels, in an aim to underline the consequences of stepping outside their expected role. Even the female sex role within relationships was demonstrated as a target of criticism, essentially reflecting the sexual power of young men and the submissive role of young women as sexual beings. The young women who wanted sex, or demonstrated their overt sexual desires outside the remit of a relationship, were also shamed into hiding their desires, which is in sharp contrast to the 'laddish' Facebook pages, which were used to humiliate young women, circulate photos and stories and rate these women based on their physical appearance. The young women who did participate in sex or demonstrated a desire for sex were often openly humiliated.

The responses to the statement that 'Girlfriends should always be sexually available to their boyfriends', yielded 90 per cent disagreement, with only 5 per cent agreeing with this view (5 per cent noted 'I don't know'), illustrating their attitudes towards consent. Aleysha described the dilemma: "If you don't have sex with them, they won't want you". She said that she had been open to having sex and now felt that "she didn't respect herself then", but that "When you say 'no', they say 'fuck off then if you're not going to do that'" and went on to note that she now realises that "sex means a lot, but for some boys it's not – it's just a shag". This dilemma has far-reaching concerns for young people's well-being, in particular, around the understanding of sexual consent as an 'active and continuing consent model' (Coy, Kelly, Vera-Gray, Garner and Kanyeredzi, 2016) rather than one focused on promoting 'no means no'. The 'emotional bracketing' coding in the transcripts reflect that Aleysha was 'matter of fact' when discussing her experiences, with her tone of voice becoming harsh and her body language closed as she normalised this form of behaviour. Her body language illustrated her discomfort with her position; she demonstrated the confusion and the impact of sex as making her feel guilty, dirty and regretful. Not only did this reflect her dilemma, it also indicated the impact on her self-esteem and well-being, reflecting confusion of identity and value of self.

Reflections: diverging paths of attitudes and experiences

This discussion contributes to the existing debates on the dominant discourses about female sexuality, which ultimately give rise to the structural foundation that supports the existence of harmful behaviour within young intimate relationships. While the participants demonstrated an attitude of zero tolerance towards any form of abuse, as reflected in the ideas shared during the advisory groups and highlighted within the questionnaire findings, these attitudes did not transfer to their 'lived experiences' of their online or offline relationships. There was a general disconnect between attitudes, beliefs and the reality of their narratives. Young women have limited power or control with reference to their sexuality within their intimate relationships. Their general attitudes and beliefs towards gendered norms and equality reflected a rejection of essentialism and the ideology of the breadwinning male and housewife. However, this perspective was mostly invisible in their narratives, even within relationships perceived as 'healthy' or 'good'. It can be argued that barriers preventing the operationalisation of their attitudes, beliefs, wishes and feelings reinforced gender differences, providing unstable grounding for a change towards 'real' gender equality. The findings from the questionnaire and the interviews diverged, with the journey on both paths revealing an image of young women unable to draw on a narrative of choice in order to assert their individual needs or negotiate their predetermined relationship scripts.

While the young women on the whole were able to name, label and isolate abusive behaviours within the questionnaire, they subsequently justified various forms of abuse, both observed and experienced within their everyday lives, during the interview stage of this study. Their perspectives on their actual sexual power widely digressed from their attitudes towards power imbalances in their own intimate relationships. Indeed, some forms of behaviour were viewed as acceptable, 'OK' or justified in particular circumstances. This was in sharp contrast to the questionnaire findings, which illustrated that over half of the sample positioned themselves within a framework of equality, believing that unequal power and control sustained abusive behaviours within intimate relationships. Their narratives revealed the confusing and often contradictory challenges faced when negotiating their sexual identities. Overall, this outlines the limited interpersonal power held by young women. For example, Glain saw it as positive that she had modified her behaviour to become "subtle". This essentially meant that she managed her appearance and behaviour in a manner that was socially desirable. She did not see her need for subtlety as a hindrance, but rather as a necessary expectation of being a young woman seeking respect, subsequently qualifying her actions as "but I'm weird". In reality, their position and power appeared constrained within their narratives about their actual relationships. Their inability to operationalise their attitudes on an 'everyday' basis is crucial to understanding the nature of their relationships and in shaping future prevention and support mechanisms. The young women did not describe themselves as vulnerable; rather, their narratives illustrated their lack of power and influence within their own intimate relationships. Furthermore, they overwhelmingly illustrated 'double standards' perspectives regarding female and male sexuality and sexualisation. These 'double standards' framed the environment which allowed the presence and growth of a pattern of abusive behaviour. As such, there was a general lack of genuine or real understanding of both the individual and structural levels of inequalities.

5

The nature of online abuse

The use of social media has changed the nature of communication in relationships and is integral in shaping the landscape of young people's peer and intimate relationships. The COVID-19 global pandemic has further raised the need for daily virtual communication during periods of national lockdowns, due to restricted space and rights to meet on a face-to-face basis. There is an increasingly blurred line between the 'online' and 'offline' contexts of all relationships but, in particular, intimate relationships. Mobiles and social networking are fundamental elements of young peoples' relationships, with online and offline symmetries in control mechanisms and distinct forms of online exploitation identified. Rapid developments in social media technologies further perpetuate this trend, with the use and ownership of various social media tools necessary to facilitate the dominant digital social communication of everyday life. As the nature of interpersonal communication has shifted with the widespread use of the internet and mobile phones, so has the possibility for emotional abuse, specifically, the ability to monitor movements. Not only has social media ensured that information is easily accessible, it has also provided a means for surveillance and constant communication.

The social media and internet era has brought its uses and limitations for young people. The use of social media invades all aspects of everyday life through the continued use of it to form online/offline relationships, very much pervasive for the new media generation. Evidence suggests that, while young people can access good quality sexual health information, they are also increasingly accessing sexually explicit and pornographic material (Tanton et al, 2015). Research has highlighted the regularity of exposure and access to pornography, with young men generally viewing it positively (Martellozzo et al, 2016), while it has been argued that young women view its consumption as uncomfortable and distasteful (Horvath et al, 2013). Significant concerns have also been identified regarding the coercive nature of teenage relationships and the confusion between 'caring' and 'controlling' behaviour (Barter et al, 2009), further perpetuated by 'sexting' and the frequent viewing of pornography (Stanley et al, 2016), reflecting wider sexual pressures. The continued exposure and gendered consumption of pornography maintains both sexist attitudes and sexual coercion through its unrealistic and unloving image of sex (Flood, 2009). Seeing, believing and striving towards the sexual standards/images of porn serve as a masculine measure of proving sexual knowledge (Martellozzo et al, 2016). However, in reality, pornography only serves to further oppress and restrict sexual liberation due to its unrealistic depiction of sex. Equally, a distressing factor is young men's tendency to turn to pornography to learn about sex, in particular, their use of it as a manual for sexual relationships (Coy, 2013), which is concerning, particularly when consideration is given to the non-engagement of key issues, such as consent. Therefore, the dilemma of the internet, with its ability to perpetuate abuse by functioning as a platform to facilitate bullying behaviour, grooming and the non-consensual circulation of sensitive sexual images, can equally function as a supportive tool with vast information privately at young women's fingertips. The function of mobiles and social networking are fundamental elements of young peoples' relationships, with online and offline symmetries in control mechanisms and distinct forms of online exploitation identified in the young women's narratives. The use of Facebook, Snapchat and so-called 'spy apps' also perpetuate the cycle of online abuse and coercive control. Within this increased era of online identities, online control and surveillance is accepted as normal by many young people (Barter et al, 2015), including revenge porn and the non-consensual circulation of images.

The influence of social media on young people's intimate relationships was evident across this age group. At the start of the advisory groups, several techniques were used to encourage participation. An icebreaker was arranged to introduce young people to the advisory group setting. The exercise asked participants in small groups to imagine that a yacht had been arranged to transport them to a desert island for two weeks. However, they were asked to visualise the island and decide which three items they would take with them. This 'icebreaker' proved popular in establishing the tone of the group and also the 'fun' aspect of discussing ideas. However, the outcome of this discussion had wider implications for the research design as the key items selected for the trip were iPhones or iPads. Being able to continue offline relationships was imperative for them, as they separated their three items into a social media device, a charger and a Wi-Fi connection. This selection of items was virtually universally adopted for each group across both advisory groups, taking priority over practical items, toiletries, friends and family. When probed further about their choices, the consensus was that social media devices were key tools in establishing and maintaining relationships, but also in keeping them 'in the loop'. This discussion reaffirmed the need to embed questions about the use of social media in young intimate relationships throughout the research tools. This was at the expense of taking a family member or friend with them, or indeed having access to food and water! Of those surveyed, 90.3 per cent owned a mobile phone with internet access, again reaffirming the importance of continuous access to the internet, with the majority of young women without internet access on their phone in the lower end of the sample age range, and only five young women aged 17–18 years old without internet access on their phone. The most popular social media tool was their own mobile phone, followed by the iPad and the PC, with young women gaining both personal and household access to devices.

Participants valued their 'online' internet access so as to maintain and continue their 'offline' relationships and friendships. The dominance of social media sites was highlighted due to their prevalent use, with 83.3 per cent accessing Facebook and 75 per cent using Snapchat. Other sites were also favourites, for example, Twitter, WhatsApp and Tumblr. However, despite this visible presence of social media, only 16.6 per cent of the sample stated that they used webcams when communicating online. Despite this low percentage, during the planning stage, several schools noted that they had encountered cases of the inappropriate use of webcams, which had caused child protection concerns. For example, one school reported concerns that a young woman in year 12 had been exposing herself online through the use of a webcam to groups of older men. The notions of social media communication and sexting as risky behaviours were evident in the concerns articulated across the schools, with young women often creating false social media personas. Another key issue was the non-consensual circulation of sensitive pictures and the creation of these often without consent, which will be discussed later in this chapter.

Gender norms, online control and surveillance

It is important to explore the link between gender roles and the use of social media as both a communication and surveillance tool. One of the statements in the survey asked the young women to rate whether 'Girlfriends should be available to answer texts and Facebook messages all the time, but boyfriends can do as they please'. A high percentage (92 per cent) of the sample 'strongly disagreed/disagreed' with this statement. Overall, just over 3 per cent of participants 'agreed' with this statement. Not only does this illustrate an attitude of rejecting the view that girlfriends should be constantly available but it further shows the response of participants towards statements challenging their perceived equal role within relationships, primarily, that they should always be available while boys/young men enjoyed freedom of 'doing as they please'.

Despite this, the actual relationship narratives of the young women illustrated their experiences of feeling that they should be available for their boyfriends as and when required. This would often be dictated by their boyfriends to their own inconvenience. For example, though Claire described her relationship as loving and stable, she portrayed one incident following a change to their relationship routine. She had travelled to another part of Wales with the school and had stayed in accommodation with limited mobile phone reception and Wi-Fi access. As a result, she had been unable to contact her boyfriend, as arranged. The consequence was "his mood", explicitly, a feeling of jealousy and insecurity by her boyfriend, which subsequently triggered a verbal argument due to her lack of availability and presence on social media. Across the sample, there was a general expectation of being in touch and reporting movements. The consequence of not adhering to this limitation in space and social networks was also evident through the consequence of 'his mood'. The availability of social media networks made surveillance practices more overt and accessible. Several participants described how their social media presence would be monitored, in particular, the status and pictures shown on social media threads. However, while this form of monitoring would often be undertaken covertly and without their girlfriends' knowledge, the constant text messages and phone calls were a vehicle used to explicitly disturb and disrupt social freedom. The fear and threat of using social media to not only monitor movements but also to humiliate and punish young women was evident. This overt display of abusive behaviour is contrary to the hidden nature of adult abusive behaviours, indicating a lack of awareness of acceptable behaviours, or the need to hide this harmful display.

Participants disagreed with the belief that young women should be 'available' more than their boyfriends to answer text and Facebook messages. A statement in the survey asked whether 'Boyfriends who text and phone their girlfriends all day are just being caring'. The highest percentage of participants disagreed with this statement (31.4 per cent), followed by 30 per cent selecting 'I don't know'. The polar end of the scale was similar, with 7.3 per cent strongly disagreeing, while 7.7 per cent strongly agreed with this statement. However, 23.6 per cent agreed with this statement, demonstrating that just under a quarter of participants observed this as caring. This demonstrates attitudes accepting of behaviour that does not explicitly appear to be abusive but could be a form of control or surveillance, illustrating the confusion between caring and potentially controlling behaviour. When asked whether the use or surveillance of someone's social media use, identity and presence without consent was abusive, 61.6 per cent saw this form of behaviour as abusive. The permission of free access to check your partner's phone was also a contentious issue with young men, as described by the participants, with their boyfriends often portrayed as overprotective of their own privacy, but wanting free access to check their girlfriend's phone to monitor their movements, a trend observed in other research (Baker and Carreño, 2016). There were also examples of this behaviour continuing following the end of a relationship, in particular, on Facebook, where photos would be 'liked' or comments placed on old statuses, which stimulated jealousy. Although this form of behaviour was visible and explicit, young women interviewed discussed their feelings and concerns when they saw a photo/selfie of their boyfriends close to another girl. There was a general view that if you were in a relationship, you had to modify your behaviour, in particular, if you were in a photo and it was posted on Facebook. However, the young women's reactions to these photos/selfies were described as different from their boyfriends', with their overall tendency to be not to react or say anything for fear of triggering an argument or explicitly sharing their jealous feelings, as it was perceived as a sign of insecurity and 'neediness'. These feelings continued to remain hidden as the relationship progressed. As Donna explained: "With pictures on Facebook ... he's more jealous with certain people, but I'm generally jealous with everyone. Before, I would have said something, but now I don't". This suggests a broader and gendered view of jealousy, with jealousy naturalised as an entitlement for young men but a feeling that should not be shared by young women.

The fear and threat of using social media to not only monitor movements but also to humiliate and punish young women was evident. This overt display of abusive behaviour is contrary to the hidden nature of adult abusive behaviours, indicating a lack of awareness of acceptable behaviours or the need to hide this harmful display. While this may indicate the visibility of verbal abuse in young intimate relationships, it also reflects that young people are socialised in order to display these types of behaviour in the public arena, showing the normalisation of verbal and emotional abuse. As a result, the visibility of this behaviour does not appear to function as a protective factor, despite the risks associated with the 'hidden' aspect of abusive behaviours within adult intimate relationships. This aspect requires specific consideration when designing prevention programmes, in particular, the role of peers in identifying abuse and providing suitable support (see Chapter 7 for further discussion on this point).

Sending 'nudies' and 'nudes'

Sexting is the practice of sending sexual images via text or instant messaging; however, the term 'sexting' is an adult term, illustrating the gulf in adult discourse and young people's 'everyday' lives (Ringrose et al, 2012). Despite the relative paucity of empirical data on sexting, much debate focuses on its negative gendered impact (Phippen, 2012; Ringrose et al, 2012; Wood et al, 2015), whereby there is a higher likelihood that young women will be the recipients of these unsolicited messages (Ringrose et al, 2012). There are links to the sexualisation of young people, specifically young women (Ringrose et al, 2012; Renold, 2013). Research indicates that 12 per cent of 11–16 year olds (Ringrose, 2012) have received sexual images online, with a change in prevalence rate with age, as younger children/young people (11–12 year-olds) are less likely to receive these images, though less change is observed with class status (Livingstone et al, 2010; Ringrose et al, 2012). Unwanted sexual activity has extended to the virtual sphere, with a high prevalence rate of engagement of young people in unwanted sexting with relationship partners (Drouin and Tobin, 2014; Drouin, Ross and Tobin, 2015). The terms frequently used by the young women to describe 'sexting' were interchangeable and complex, primarily, focused on key words, such as sending 'nudies' or 'nudes', within the culture of sexual bullying online. Sexting can be a consensual and desired element of friendships and intimate relationships. Hasinoff (2015) argues that young people's capacity for choice should be realised when debating about 'sexting panic', and, in particular, the need to educate about consent. Hasinoff offers practical advice and an alternative view of sexting beyond its potential risk for young people. However, sexting in certain circumstances is harmful and linked to GBV, for example, when young men and men constantly request 'nudies/selfies',[1] rate physical appearance and share images of young women without their consent. These images can also remain in the virtual world indefinitely, resulting in this harm being visible online for an indefinite period (Henry, Flynn and Powell, 2020).

This research revealed that the pattern of use of social media evolved with age, with the younger groups using primarily Snapchat, and the use of Facebook often substituted for Tinder in time. Sexting was also seen as the norm, and indeed a trend for year 9 and 10 pupils. The younger women within the sample who did not have relationship experience appeared more reflective than those within their year group who did in fact have relationship experience. They also appeared less tolerant of the non-consensual circulation of social media images and unwanted rating of body parts. Collette commented: "Personally, I wouldn't have a relationship with a boy who mails pictures. It's more about pictures these days". However, within established older relationships, social media was used as a coercive tool in order to monitor virtual relationships and check online behaviour, for example, the 'likes' on Facebook pictures, the change in Facebook relationship status and the practice by young people of 'blocking' individuals from their girlfriend's/boyfriend's page. There were also examples of different expectations of behaviour online and offline, for example, the dilemma of acting in a passive or 'subtle' manner offline and revealing and sharing 'nudie' photos online. Their power in navigating the uncharted territory of young intimate relationships was limited and complex through online platforms. The idea of 'image-based sexual abuse' has been conceptualised as the non-consensual making and sharing of private sexual images, which should be situated on a continuum of sexual violence in order to ensure sufficient connection with a broad spectrum of sexual violence, harassment, gender norms, victim blaming attitudes, choice and consent (McGlynn and Rackley, 2017; McGlynn et al, 2017). Recent research reflects the experiences of young people of 'image-based sexual abuse', in particular, how sexual images and messages can be used to inflict humiliation and control (Stanley et al, 2016). Sexual peer pressure via social media is more prevalent than online 'stranger danger' (Ringrose et al, 2012), with a growing trend of sharing indecent images on mobiles acknowledged.

The next section of the survey explored attitudes towards 'lad culture', which is defined as 'overt sexism' (Sundaram and Jackson, 2015, p 2). The concept of 'lad culture' or 'laddism' has been described as a form of masculinity which illustrates behaviour traits focused on sexism, competitiveness and misogyny that has significant socio-cultural power, while impacting on identity and experience (Phipps and Young, 2015). The specific statement on the survey exploring this issue asked whether 'Rating the appearance of girls on social media is just a bit of fun'. The statement was phrased in order to question whether this behaviour was acceptable or justified if framed as 'just for a laugh', or worded here as a 'just bit of fun'. Just under 70 per cent of participants 'strongly disagreed/disagreed' with this statement, with less than 10 per cent reflecting some form of agreement. However, just under a quarter of participants (21.4 per cent) said that they 'didn't know' and were therefore unsure of their opinion, either on this form of behaviour or whether or not it could be 'just a bit of fun'. This degree of ambivalence illustrates the potential confusion between their roles, the pressure of the system of 'rating' as popularity currency, the monitoring of their appearance and the increasing prevalence of practices focused on posting and circulating sexualised pictures. This form of behaviour is also often linked to popularity, acceptance and exposure. This mirrors social norms that men display humour, while women are expected to laugh and enjoy these jokes irrespective of their content, as women are seen to have a 'sense of humour' if they respond to and appreciate it, rather than use humour themselves. This reflects the link to gendered double standards and the consequences of negative exposure.

When asked whether they felt that further information or support on how social media shows sex and relationships was required, only 25 per cent responded that this would be useful, while 53.2 per cent noted that this was not necessary and 21.8 per cent replied 'I don't know'. The experiences described within the young women's relationship narratives around sexting or 'nudies' were primarily focused on sexual inclusion/exclusion, consent and control. Indeed, within particular schools, the presence of coercive social media groups was evident and problematic. For example, social media 'laddish' groups were established to share sexualised banter and rate the appearance of young women within their school. One particular group was labelled as 'the lads', a trend observed by the researcher and further reiterated by both teacher and participants across the schools, sometimes packaged differently but nonetheless equally problematic and sexist. The analysis of the young women's narratives revealed the full complexity of this behaviour, which was described in contradictory terms by participants as desired, unwanted, coercive, sexual and accidental.

It was common practice within the schools for groups of young men (GSCE age range) to rate the physical appearance of their female peers on Facebook pages, with these pages often labelled as the 'LADS' page, in keeping with laddish behaviour (Phipps and Young, 2015). Also, the use of texting shifted with age, with requests for nudies and sexting a key trend with pupils within the GSCE age range. The practice around requesting 'nudies' was highly gendered and coercive. Interestingly, for the young women, responding to nudie requests was permissible, and part of the sexual culture or expectations of the peer group. As illustrated, initiating this behaviour or establishing the boundaries of permissible online sexual relationships was not. This was shown by the disgust shared about a young woman who requested nudies from young men and later 'had fun' in saving them in a personal folder. However, the idea that young men automatically and randomly send photos of their penises around their peer group was labelled as "they have no shame; it's just a boy thing to do" (Aleysha). In contrast to the expected norm of sexual restraint offline, young women were required to be visually 'sexy' online.

Glain described how she had received a plethora of requests for 'nudies' one evening; she felt pressurised, reflecting that young women are often coerced to take a naked selfie or video. She decided to tackle these unwanted requests by first peeling an apple and then sending a picture of the 'naked' apple. As the requests continued, she took a photo of a bath sponge and declared it as a nudie of SpongeBob.[2] There was a sense of an underlying threat of embarrassment if behaviour contravened social norms, illustrating the social control and expectation that young women collude to sustain their continued subordination of their sexuality. As reflected by Glain, steps had to be taken to modify her behaviour in order to avoid embarrassment and shame, but this was done with a sense of humour in order to deflect these unwanted requests in a creative manner. This modification ensured the maintenance of social hierarchies and established power dynamics. Glain demonstrated her own surveillance of her position and behaviour to ensure that she was "subtle" and conformed to normative gender standards in order to avoid judgement or an unwanted label. She reinforced the "subtle" choices *she* makes and the attention she pays to the actions of others when deciding the boundaries of permissible sexual behaviour for herself. This is further reinforced by the lack of discussion within the interviews of female sexual pleasure and desire, illustrating the missing discourse of desire (Fine, 1988).

'Revenge pornography' involves the circulation of nude or partially nude photos or videos without the person's consent, with a plethora of broad academic definitions provided for this relatively new phenomenon. There are also debates across the literature that this non-consensual circulation of images or videos occurs within the context of a breakdown of an intimate relationship (Walker and Sleath, 2017). While the 'revenge' element links to the notion of a relationship breakdown, there are several examples drawn from the interviews that demonstrate that defining this issue as a broader form of sexual harm (DeKeseredy and Schwartz, 2016) on a continuum of technology-facilitated abusive behaviour would be more suitable (as suggested by McGlynn et al, 2017), specifically, as the continued circulation of an image and reaction to this act is often sustained by a wider peer group. Not only were there examples of surveillance by checking phone and social media content but also, again, the reinforcement of social media as a humiliation tool. Examples were also shared of revenge porn being instigated and facilitated by ex-boyfriends; for example, a young woman who cheated on her boyfriend was upset when her ex-boyfriend shared 'nudies' of her on Facebook and Snapchat without her consent. In another case, Glain described how her friend's boyfriend "leaked" nude photos of his girlfriend/Glain's friend as a result of her choice to have a night out with her friends, whom he labelled as 'sluts'. It's interesting that Glain described this as the photo being "leaked", rather than being explicit that this private photo had been shared without consent. As a consequence, Glain's friend had to create a new Facebook page. Glain reported that her boyfriend's surveillance subsequently resulted in sexual coercion and his refusal to allow her to leave his house until she had sex with him, at which point her friends intervened and demanded that she left his property with them.

Reflections

As illustrated in this discussion, a key concern drawn from the data is the general focus of blame and judgement on the young women whose images were circulated without their consent. The gendered nature of this harm is highlighted by the fact that several studies indicate that young men perpetrate this form of abuse more than young women (Walker and Sleath, 2017), with a significant negative impact on the mental health and well-being of survivors of this form of harm documented (Bates, 2017). Overall, the views shared by the young women reflect the use of social media as a tool used to control their physical movements, emotional well-being and bodies. Their physical movements could be monitored 24/7, with the threat of this surveillance often sufficient control to restrict their social lives and interactions with others. Their bodies, sexual identities and reputations were controlled through the non-consensual sharing of images, and also through the constant bombardment of requests for 'nudies'. This reinforced the stigma and shame attached to the way they negotiated their virtual or online identities. Discussing how 'subtle' they should remain in order to avoid judgement felt exhausting, in particular, as this online era now ensures that this is perpetuated at a click of a button, at any time, anywhere in the world.

Promoting healthy relationships: a whole-community approach

The focus of this chapter is on drawing upon the research findings to inform the development of prevention and early intervention education with young people in schools and beyond. The chapter outlines an overview of current sex and relationship or healthy relationship education, primarily delivered in educational settings. The discussion also offers a practical approach to preventing and addressing this issue across communities on a whole-system basis. Essentially, it is argued that any preventative programme delivered should be accompanied by appropriate referral, assessment, safety planning systems and robust evaluation.

The focus of prevention education for young people should be on recognising the impact of everyday forms of GBV as a continuum of naturalised harassment and abuse of women by men, rather than as a 'sledgehammer', or abuse perpetrated by a minority of dominant men (Stanko, 1985). Young people should be educated on understanding the impact of everyday harassment and abuse experienced by known perpetrators from their own intimate relationships, and therefore a focus should be on understanding young people's lived experiences of relationship abuse. Young women should be educated on the norms associated with women's gendered roles, specifically, young men's power and entitlement to young women's bodies, their feelings and thoughts. The foundation of prevention education with young people should focus on normative gendered power dynamics and its impact on their experiences of the everyday routines of their intimate relationships, including the established scripts of the progression of their relationships, how they experience intimacy, coercion and abuse and how these experiences differ as a result of their individual needs, well-being and personal profiles, therefore identifying the connections in the ways that young women experience abuse within their intimate relationships, while also identifying the impact of their individualised needs on their own subjective experiences.

Building on the state of current sex and relationship education in the UK, the focus of this chapter is on exploring the idea of gendered social norms as the foundation of prevention and early intervention education across communities. The discussion will also include an emphasis on the impact of peer and professional relationships in supporting young people within their intimate relationships. The chapter will finalise with concentrating on the need to develop a policy on 'healthy relationship' education that utilises a 'whole-community approach' that includes a focus on tackling gender norms as its foundation. This policy should go beyond the school setting in order to incorporate key multi-agency stakeholders, parents/ carers and the wider community as a whole. The recommendation is that normative gendered power dynamics and their impact on the experiences of the everyday routines of young women's intimate relationships, including the established scripts of the progression of these relationships, how they experience intimacy, coercion and abuse and how these experiences differ as a result of their individual needs and well-being, should be a form of foundation of preventative education, thus identifying the connections in the ways that young women experience abuse within their relationships, while also identifying the impact of their individualised intersecting needs on their own subjective experiences. The foundation of prevention education should focus on empowering young women as 'active agents' who have the power to operationalise their attitudes and beliefs as part of their intimate relationships.

This chapter argues that effective prevention education is required in schools, not only to prevent abuse in intimate relationships but also to challenge established heteronormative roles which inform relationship expectations and the notion of 'what's OK' and 'not OK' in teenage relationships. This argument is offered in response to the narratives of the young women interviewed, and their overall lack of power to operationalise non-hierarchical gendered relations within intimate lives. This was despite their ability to clearly articulate their perceived healthy attitudes towards gender equality. Prevention education needs to have a practical focus on providing young women with the ability to apply their understanding of relationship equality to their reality, while preparing young men to relinquish their power and privilege. Furthermore, the young women's narratives revealed a lack of understanding of what it means to operationalise equality in intimate relationships in order to have equal power.

Recent debates on prevention education

A review of the global perspective of sex/health relationship education provides an eclectic approach to addressing this issue across diverse cultures and communities. Across the US, there is general support for sex education in schools, with 96 per cent of parents supporting sex education in high schools (Planned Parenthood, 2021). However, the models of sex/relationship education are focused on state- or local-level provision, as there is no federal law that outlines a prescriptive direction for sex education in schools and communities. This results in the provision across the US being framed by the local culture, attitudes and politics. Therefore, what is taught and included in programmes is decided by state laws across the US, meaning an unstable foundation for inclusive and consistent sex education provision.

The nature and focus of programmes vary significantly, from those advocating 'abstinence-only-until-marriage sex education' or sexual risk avoidance programmes, to more inclusive ones focusing on promoting healthy relationships and preventing dating violence (CDC, 2021). There are progressive programmes available, for example, 'Dating Matters', which is a preventative programme focused on the whole system of working with individuals, peers, families, schools and neighbourhoods (CDC, 2018). A recent evaluation reflects the promise of this programme, in particular, the ecological foundation of the model (Debnam and Temple, 2021). As a result of a broad spectrum of programmes, sex and healthy relationships prevention programmes are often polarised in the US, with a call that this limited focus needs a re-focus on gender, sexuality and sexual pleasure (Kantor and Lindberg, 2020). The lack of consistent available information in Canada has made it a challenge to have a clear perspective of the nature of education provision offered across the country. This illustrates the importance of gathering data and evaluating programmes. The available Canadian data illustrates the approach adopted is often outdated, with a narrow focus on health outcomes (Action Canada for Sexual Health and Rights, 2019). In Australia, young people's perspectives are captured every five years through the national survey of students and sexual health. The landscape across Australia also shows the mixed perspective towards sex and relationship education, with a recent survey reflecting that young people want engaging sex and relationship education that focuses on a broad spectrum of age-appropriate content (Fisher et al, 2019).

International bodies (for example, the World Health Organization [WHO]) have outlined key objectives expected of EU Members when designing and delivering sexuality education. The Standards for Sexuality Education were implemented by the WHO in 2010, with the UN sustainable goals focused on promoting healthy lives and well-being, ensuring the equitable provision of education and empowering young women. In addition, UNESCO (2009) outlined eight key concepts that should shape the focus of sexuality education, including relationships; values, rights, culture and sexuality; understanding gender; violence and staying safe; skills for health and well-being; the human body and development; sexuality and sexual behaviour; and sexual and reproductive health. The European Commission (2020) undertook a review of what was termed 'sexuality education' (sexual and reproductive health) across the European Union, illustrating the lack of mapping of provisions across Europe. As a result, this limits our understanding of the nature of provision and 'what works' well or requires further development. However, the report clearly outlines that specific countries adopt a biological focus to this education (for example,

Cyprus, Italy, Slovenia and Romania), while others adopt an emphasis on risk prevention (Bulgaria, Croatia, Czech Republic, Ireland and Lithuania) (European Commission, 2020, p 7). From a European perspective, the Dutch approach offers insight into a progressive and much more inclusive culture towards sex and relationship education. The statutory Dutch model begins at pre-school level, and covers a broad spectrum of topics in a positive manner, including love, identity and sexuality (de Melker, 2015), with an attitude focused on continual improvement to the curriculum. Therefore, a brief summary of programmes across the globe reflects inconsistency and a general lack of data evaluating approaches adopted that are both diverse and inclusive of a plethora of needs across communities.

Bringing the discussion back to the UK, following the delay in implementing the Domestic Abuse Bill in England and Wales, there was a general paucity in the debate around the statutory provision of healthy relationship education. Charities working with young people expressed concerns of the gaps in sex education teaching, in particular, the lack of focus on teaching the importance of 'sexual consent' (NCB, 2016) and 'respect' within young people's intimate relationships. The debate continued in England,[1] albeit on an uncertain and acrimonious platform. The development of what was known as 'sex education' across the UK has followed an arduous path due to the level of debate, disagreement and contention. This debate was focused on several key issues, including whether the responsibility of teaching children about sex education should solely lie with parents/carers. The degree of work and, indeed, activism to transform the traditional 'sex education' model to focus more on progressive issues, such as exploring respectful, equal and healthy intimate relationships, should not be underestimated. On a positive note, the level of public consultation, engagement and degree of co-production to gather a broad spectrum of views from a plethora of stakeholders to inform these new developments is a key achievement. We have now reached a stage where each part of the UK has followed its own path in developing a curriculum to focus on this specific area of teaching and learning. In England, relationships education is now compulsory in all primary schools, with sex education mandatory in all secondary schools, and health education compulsory in all state-funded schools, with personal, social, health and economic education (PSHE) continuing to be compulsory in independent schools. While the focus on teaching this subject area is on exploring healthy and respectful relationships, with teaching on mental well-being also central to these subjects, the English guidance also outlines the rights of parents/carers to withdraw pupils from some or all of the sex education teaching (not relationships or health education).

The focus on the new approach to sex education teaching aligns with the key principles of the Equality Act 2010, to ensure equity to all students, with the aim of concentrating the teaching and learning on diverse issues of identity, sexuality and equality. The emphasis is on placing a degree of responsibility on schools to role model positive behaviours that challenge everyday sexism, misogyny, homophobia and gender stereotypes. Guidance should highlight the importance of working with parents/carers and the wider community, in particular, around effective communication regarding teaching content, delivery and parental rights. Guidance should also make reference to the requirement for a flexible approach that is responsive to local public health, specific community issues and situated within a whole-school approach, which aligns with later discussion in this chapter on the whole-community approach.

Exploring media campaigns

An example of a prevention campaign aimed at tackling abuse in young people's relationships is the Home Office This Is Abuse campaign. The Home Office commissioned two separate media campaigns (This Is Abuse, 2010–2015), one in February 2010 at a cost of £2 million and the second in September 2011 at a cost of £1.5 million. The focus was on targeting young people aged 13–18 by encouraging them to evaluate their views on abuse, violence and consent within intimate relationships. The campaign was also included as part of the teen soap opera Hollyoaks, and was shown on MTV, which also included several adverts with high-profile celebrities. Social marketing has been a key component of domestic abuse prevention work with young people, owing to the ability of this method of communication to reach young people, due to their familiarity with the use of social media. Implementing expensive media campaigns, while at the same time rejecting the debate around compulsory healthy relationship education in all schools, was troubling, in particular, due to the growing concern at the time around the content, quality and impact of PSHE teaching (Ofsted, 2013). The lack of clarity and the challenges faced by this type of education is summarised well by Allen (2008): 'sexuality education is a site of competing political interests, comprising parents/caregivers, teachers, school management, educational policy makers, civil liberty organizations, conservative and liberal groups' (p 574).

The This Is Abuse video clips illustrated individual stories, with the onus on the audience to select the possible options available to the perpetrator and victim from both standpoints (whether to stop the abuse or not), by asking the audience to reflect on their views on the possible options available. This campaign remained focused on individualised notions of risk and responsibility, rather than the broader gendered norms that scaffold such abusive behaviours. While these forms of video clips/media campaigns do have a place in raising awareness of this type of abuse, as discussed earlier with reference to Kelly's continuum and Stanko's view of the sledgehammer intrusion concept, such campaigns and scenarios should concentrate on reflecting on the influence of structural inequality, power and control and on the abusive dynamics in intimate relationships.

Gadd et al's (2014) analysis of the This Is Abuse Bedroom video clip was conducted as part of the Boys to Men research project,[2] with the analysis of this specific video clip discussed as part of the focus groups conducted. For the analysis, they concentrated on the discussion with three young men who participated in the focus groups, as these were known to be perpetrators of violence against women because they were being supervised by the Youth Offending Team. By focusing on the views of these three young men, the attention is diverted towards known perpetrators, rather than on the views of a broader range of young people. This suggested the contradictory identifications for the young people viewing the This Is Abuse video clips (specifically, the 'Bedroom' video[3]), with both anti-violence messages and victim-blaming discourses identified. They questioned the potential 'boomerang effect' of this prevention campaign: the risk that the message from the video clips would have the opposite impact of that intended, specifically, that the young men viewing the clips sympathise with the perpetrators of the abuse. The gendered element of this form of abuse was missing both in the young men's discussion and also as part of their analysis.

The focus of the analysis illustrated by Gadd et al (2014) is on how these three young men excuse and justify the abusive behaviour of the young man in the video, rather than on the structural power and control of men that sustains this form of abuse, while they acknowledge that social marketing campaigns should not be the key or 'standalone' component of domestic abuse preventative work with young men, due to the complexity of the fluid attitudes of these men who are known perpetrators often ostracised in society. The discussion doesn't include the fact that preventative work needs to be universal, accessed by all young people, with broad content that includes an emphasis on the impact of structural inequality, and a spectrum of attitudes and experiences of young people. Despite the positive outcomes measured by the Home Office (2015) in their evaluation of this campaign, the campaign did have problems, as no pre-testing on the knowledge and attitudes of the young people viewing the clips had been undertaken prior to it.

Following the This Is Abuse campaign, a new one, DISRESPECT NOBODY,[4] was launched by the Home Office in 2016 through the release of online and TV adverts, with the aim of tackling sexting, relationship abuse, consent, porn and rape, with an overall focus on healthy relationships. This campaign built on the learning of This Is Abuse and had the aim of covering a broader range of topics, with a focus on healthy relationships rather than abuse per se. The website included information on each of these topics, including video clips, individual real-life stories, PHSE teaching materials and information for young people on how they could access advice and support. Based on the limitations of measuring the impact of This Is Abuse, it may prove challenging to measure the exact impact of media campaigns on long-term attitude shifts and behavioural change (Home Office, 2015). While a full evaluation of this campaign is yet to be released, in contrast to the This Is Abuse evaluation, the focus of the DISRESPECT NOBODY assessment will be on measuring the pre- and post-campaign awareness, engagement and impact on attitudes and behaviours of a target audience in order to continually improve and amend the campaign. As mentioned, while marketing campaigns can be useful in raising awareness and offering initial education on sensitive topics, which can be viewed within a private space, long-term impact and behavioural change can only be achieved by adopting a more sustained approach of prevention education.

Developing prevention education

The need to implement evidence-based domestic abuse/healthy relationship interventions aimed particularly at young people in the UK is now acknowledged (for example, EVAWG, 2021 Home Office, 2013; Estyn, 2017; Renold and McGeeney, 2017). Evidence from the US already illustrates the positive impact of several healthy relationship programmes (for example, Safe Dates and LoveU2 Relationships Smart) on the prevalence of 'dating violence', in particular, around the acceptability of this form of abuse, awareness raising and demonstrating skills for conflict resolution, even when short courses were delivered (two days) (Antle et al, 2011; Foshee et al, 2004). A meta-analysis of US-based healthy relationship interventions revealed that even minor interventions can result in changing knowledge and attitudes (McLeod, Jones and Cramer, 2015). The focus should be on age-appropriate sex and relationships education which is delivered on a consistent and continuous basis (Children's Commissioner for Wales, 2013).

Evidence from the National Survey of Sexual Attitudes and Lifestyles (Natsal) reflects that the percentage of young people referring to school as their main source of information about sexual issues has steadily increased from the findings of Natsal 1 to Natsal 3, with similar percentages of men and women reporting lessons at schools as their key source of information about sex (Macdowall et al, 2015; Tanton et al, 2015). A lower level of participants reported their parents as their key source of information; however, the percentage of women acquiring information from a parent was double that of men (Macdowall et al, 2015). The findings from these studies also reflected that young people felt unprepared for their first sexual experience, as they reported they required more information, specifically, about feelings, emotions, relationships, STIs and contraception (Macdowall et al, 2015). There is a need to listen to the views of young people, with teaching sessions on healthy relationships delivered in a manner that meets the needs of a broad spectrum of these young people.

Schools are required to make sure that no gender-based discrimination exists within the institution, including ensuring equal opportunities. As discussed, schools are key sites for developing gendered identities, as described by Epstein and Johnson (1998), as schooling sexualities. Children and young people develop, define and redefine their gender identities in schools through their school work, subject choices, such as science, which continues to be conceptualised as a male subject (OECD, 2015), and other school activities (Jackson, 2005), for example, after-school clubs. Indeed, schools have been found to enable heteronormative ideas both through the curriculum and via extra-curricular practices (Ryle, 2017). Schools are the ideal socialisation sites for shaping and deterring potential harmful behaviour on a universal platform. The young women voiced their wish to have preventative and early intervention programmes integrated into their school education and to have the opportunity to talk and be listened to. Only 37.4 per cent of participants noted that they believed that there was enough information available on 'healthy relationships'. This understanding of a lack of information was expanded to other related topics, such as how social media shows sex and relationships and the meaning of consent in relationships. This is particularly pertinent when considering the messages from related research, which indicate that young people are confused about the concept of sexual consent (Burman and Cartmel, 2005). A high proportion of the sample noted that they were aware of the availability of support services on a local and national basis. This demonstrates that support services are visible, but need to tailor and target intervention to address the evolving needs of our younger generation. Also, knowing about services may not imply a willingness to discuss them.

Any work to review the state of young people's relationships, patterns of abuse and violence, gender stereotyping and sexism requires a re-examination of the role of schools in constructing gender identities and norms. This may be a challenge, as concerns have been raised that schools avoid responding to sexist behaviour and fail to understand its impact on pupils, which results in the majority of incidents of sexual harassment and sexual violence going unreported (House of Commons Equality Committee, 2016). In fact, the concerns around sexist beliefs and name calling have been evidenced in several studies; for example, 71 per cent of 16–18 year olds in schools stated that they had heard sexist name calling (slut, slag) on a daily basis, or a few times a week, with 29 per cent of young women subjected to unwanted sexual touching in schools (EVAW, 2016). Gender norms have shaped the culture of sexist banter as an everyday harmless and accepted act, not just in school but also within university or higher education settings (Sundaram and Jackson, 2015). Renold and McGeeney (2017) identify the need to eliminate sexist name calling in schools, in particular, the use of the words 'slags' and 'sluts' to describe young women, while young men were referred to as 'lads'. Not only is there a need to shift attitudes within young people's own cultures but also the expectations of teachers and caregivers, in order to eliminate stereotypical gendered norms (OECD, 2015).

As mentioned, while one-off campaigns should continue to play a role in prevention education, resources should primarily be diverted to enhance the skills available in schools to deliver programmes on a consistent basis as part of the curriculum. Recent evidence indicates that those schools that are most effective in delivering healthy relationships education do so within a culture of gender equality and respect for the rights of others (Estyn, 2017; Renold and McGeeney, 2017). A 'whole-school gender education' approach is required, which extends the 'whole-school approach' and reflects that preventative education should have a central focus on gender and gender equality in relation to violence and abuse (Sundaram, 2014, p 24), with an emphasis on the influence of gender norms in shaping young people's attitudes and experiences of abuse. The core of prevention work and early intervention work with young people should concentrate on the transformation of unequal power relationships, and the attitudes and behaviours that underpin these. As part of this prevention support, discussion on the gendered structural inequality, coercion/pressure, appropriate behaviour in respectful and consensual relationships, boundaries of personal space and specialised support should be explored. There will be further discussion on the development of a 'whole-community approach' later in this chapter.

Barriers to accessing support

Barriers to reporting domestic abuse include lack of confidence, shame and fear. As mentioned, GBV is a 'hidden' societal issue, even more so for teenagers, with them being more acceptant and dismissive of abusive behaviour patterns. The 'hidden' nature of this abuse for young people is 'in plain sight', as abusive behaviour is often nomalised and accepted. Young people's attitudes to 'barriers' primarily focused on the difficulty in leaving relationships due to perceptions of love and forgiveness, rather than practical difficulties in accessing support. Young people are more likely to report online rather than offline violence/abuse, as it appears 'easier' than direct or 'hidden' violence and abuse (Barter et al, 2015). Young women tend to identify their intimate relationships as abusive on reflection, and when the relationship has ended, specifically, when their identity is not related to their boyfriend/partner (Chung, 2005; Davies, 2019).

The provision of accessible and appropriate support and guidance for young people experiencing relationship abuse is essential, in particular, as evidence suggests that a quarter of young people suffering from relationship abuse had not told anyone (Barter et al, 2015). The young women surveyed for this present study revealed that when they intervened to support a friend who was experiencing relationship abuse, 23 per cent noted that they would ask a parent for advice, 23 per cent stated they would talk to a professional organisation, 16 per cent elected to confide in a youth worker, 11 per cent elected to discuss it with a teacher, 17 per cent noted they would choose to confide in friends rather than adults and 10 per cent stated that they would talk directly to the perpetrator of the abuse. These findings suggest that the choice of a 'sympathetic individual' was diverse and ranged from peers, family members and professional workers (youth workers, teachers) and even expanded to the online world, which indicatess that young people benefit from having a private space to seek advice and support.

This present research demonstrates the key role of parents, in particular, fathers as potential protective factors when their daughters experience abuse within intimate relationships. Lowri's relationship with an older boy was dictated by his coercive control and jealousy. She was isolated from her friends, and it was only through the intervention of her father that the relationship ended: "I would run to my dad to tell him. … If my dad would let me go back with him now, I would … when we were arguing, my dad was there for me" (Lowri). She described her wish to return to this relationship, but her father's disapproval and her wish not to disappoint him prevented her from returning to this situation. However, it is also known that fathers often regulate and police their daughters' sexuality and intimate relationships (Elliott, 2010), which impacts on the nature of discussion required with parents/carers when shaping the design and delivery of healthy relationship education in schools. Parental focus on delaying the progression of their daughters' intimate relationships was also a key theme here, much to the annoyance of Lowri, who often perceived this as misunderstanding her wishes and feelings. Several of the young women raised concerns about confiding in their parents, primarily due to their fear of disappointing them (Glesni, Chloe, Aleysha, Bella), feeling embarrassed and unable to have this form of discussion with their parents/carers (Bella, Chloe, Collette, Diane); however, they confided in their parents/carers if they were at risk of harm (Elen, Collette).

Parents/carers may require guidance, support and education in order to align their thinking with any revised curriculum/prevention programme, to support them in their parental/carer role and ensure a consistent message to their children. It is a challenge to strike a balance between the provision of support, parental control of sexual relationships and attempts to engage in numerous perceived comical discussions of young love/courtship/relationships. Specifically, some of the young women felt that their parents would 'make fun' of their relationships by teasing them. Parents/carers need to achieve a balance, or their children may fear that their discussions and questions around their intimate relationships will not be taken seriously.

Jennifer highlighted, as did others, the gap in teaching provision on healthy relationships. The impact of this gap affected the young women's choice of accessing support, as illustrated by Diane:

'There is a counsellor we can access. But we are not really told that we can talk about relationships. But we haven't had anything about healthy relationships. More to do about the health/sexual side rather than emotional side of relationships. It would be beneficial. We had a discussion the other day how it's really weird that we are now this age and there are not really that many of lessons/or session made compulsory for about what is right/wrong in a relationship.' (Diane)

Despite the visibility of a counsellor in the school, Diane notes that she did not feel able to talk to this professional about the emotional aspects of intimate relationships, as the lessons delivered on this topic had been focused on the biological aspects of these relationships. This functions as a barrier to accessing support, as young people are deterred from discussing what matters to them about relationships if the culture, the support and the school curriculum does not openly promote this dialogue on a broad spectrum of issues within young intimate relationships. This study revealed barriers and enablers for young women when attempting to access support provision. There were several barriers to accessing support/advice/guidance, primarily, the availability of professional support. The limited support services were criticised for not being person-centred or private: "You can go to school nurse. But a once a week visit is not enough as you have to queue for an appointment – it's embarrassing" (Glesni). The importance of privacy was crucial, as several young women noted that queuing for an appointment with the school nurse only served to raise questions and gossip (primarily around sex, in particular, contraception and unwanted pregnancies). So, essentially, the role of the school nurse was regarded as more focused on sex rather than relationship education/support. Bonnie expands on this issue further:

Interviewer:	Do you think something around relationships would have been quite good in school?
Bonnie:	Yeah. I don't know because with most people, if they are in one of them bad relationships, they don't exactly talk about it, no. Just like, yeah, yeah, we're OK.
Interviewer:	What do you think stops people from talking about it?
Bonnie:	Well, some of them, yeah, the boys make them think they're not good enough and they won't get anybody better than that boy and they make them feel like no

one's going to believe them, kind of thing. And it's like, yeah, basically that no one's going to believe them. It's like, no, don't be silly; just because their boyfriend's nice when they're with people, it's like, no, we couldn't do that.

Interviewer: With relationships now, in schools, what do you think would help young women? What do you think ... with regard to lessons, information, advice ... what would be helpful?

Bonnie: There's not enough sex education, to start with. Not enough support for the girls. Like, I hear about girls that are so depressed and so ... like, harming themselves. I've been through that myself and ... when I was in year 9, and I see year 9 now going through it and it's horrible. And some have been in bad relationships and it's just like they've got no one to go to. Because if they can't go to their mum, like, friends, yes, they've got their friends, but they haven't got the professional help they need. It's hard seeing the younger generation going through what they shouldn't be going through at their age.

Interviewer: What kind of specific topics do you think would be useful to learn about in lessons?

Bonnie: I think how to cope if your ... if ... how to cope with relationships if they break down or if the boy doesn't feel like you feel, if you've been heartbroken, things like that.

Interviewer: So those everyday, practical things.

Bonnie: Yeah. And how to say no, as well, because loads of girls I know do not know how to say no to boys, and it's just not right.

Interviewer: What, no to sex, or no to relationships?

Bonnie: Yeah, no to sex and to pictures. No, I won't do this.

Bonnie highlights the barrier of accessing support due to the feelings of shame and stigma of being in a "bad relationship", which again links to Goffman's concept of 'impression management' and staging the performance that 'everything's OK' in the relationship. She also illustrates how boys' impression management of being "nice" in front of others impacts on a young women's ability to access support and manipulates them to minimise the abuse experienced as being "silly" and, as a result, "no one's going to believe them". Bonnie outlines the impact on a young woman's well-being of not having access to the right professional advice and support, as this is required in addition to family and peer support. Aleysha also discussed her reluctance to ask for help due to her concerns around privacy, confidentiality and the likelihood of a breach of her confidentiality: "The support needs to be private, as you ask for support and then the school phones home".

The status and role of the professional was also important as there was a general consensus that they would not access the school child protection lead as this was often the deputy head, primarily due to their fear that the information would be shared, dealt with disproportionately and, due to their perception in one school, that the status of the deputy head, because of their role, was disengaged from the pupils. Approaching an 'outsider' appeared less daunting and more comfortable than confiding in the school nurse attached to the school: "We [young women] need someone to talk to, similar age to us, from the university, like you ... it's more beneficial to have that rather than a presentation from a professional" (Alexis). Despite the fact that I am not of a similar age to the young women who participated in this research (I was in my late 30s when I conducted the fieldwork), the learning style adopted during the study, and how I situated myself in relation to the young women, transcended the generational gap between myself as the researcher and the young women, due to the empathy adopted for their position and the provision of a confidential and private space for discussion. Alexis is essentially voicing her preference for individual support. The key concern around the role of the 'sympathetic individual' was focused on privacy, echoing the findings of recent European research (Barter et al, 2015).

There were also reflections on the quality and content of interventions received. Several young women discussed their concerns regarding interventions delivered by the police within their schools. The professional delivering this form of intervention should be suitably trained to have the appropriate qualities to facilitate a safe space for reflections and discussion on these sensitive topics. It is questionable whether the police are the appropriate agency to be delivering these forms of interventions, as their role is focused on enforcing the law. There was a general consensus that the police intervention was 'extreme', which was evidenced by their response to a police visit which revolved around the viewing of a film depicting rape:

'During the police visit, he asked, "If you are in an abusive relationship, could you get out of it?" But it's not really a question you can answer is it? He asked stupid questions. He also discussed about consent – it wasn't anything new. When you're in that type of position, it's not that easy.' (Grug)

Grug indicates her understanding of the complexities, challenges and the nuanced nature of abusive relationships. This raised several reflections around young people's confidence in the ability and suitability of specific professionals to deliver prevention sessions linked to their understanding of the key issues, for example, the barriers to accessing support in the first place. The participants did not fully comprehend the potential range of abusive behaviour, or the impact of it on their well-being, for example, the spectrum of controlling behaviour, including the surveillance, checking mobile phones/Facebook accounts, being 'in a mood' or sulking if sex was refused. This mostly went unrecognised as harmful or abusive behaviour. As a result, it often led to these abusive behaviours being normalised, justified and left unchallenged. Across the interventions, there was a general lack of attention to the continuum of abuse within intimate relationships. Messages were often gendered, with girls receiving advice focused on managing their own behaviour and being cautious. There was a general lack of discussion on gender norms, power and inequality. Grug's reflections demonstrate that care should be taken to ensure that the right intervention is offered, at the right level, by the right person, as the consequences of providing the inappropriate 'sympathetic individual' can result in provision that appears to patronise, trivialise and alienate, rather than engage, young people. This also indicates the importance of co-producing teaching materials on these topics with young people and the need to continuously evaluate the impact of prevention programmes in schools.

There was a sense from participants that there is sufficient information available on how and where to get support. Despite this, there was criticism that the support was not specialist or targeted to address their concerns, as the focus was primarily on the biological aspects of sex rather than the emotional aspects of intimate relationships. There was also a call to focus the delivery of any preventative session on practical matters, such as relationship coping strategies and supporting young people to conceptualise what is 'normal', expected or simply 'OK' in relationships.

The role of peer support

The uses and limitations of peer-led learning is also relevant to the design of prevention interventions on healthy relationships. Research has demonstrated the importance of peer relationships and support when experiencing domestic abuse (Schutt, 2006; Humphreys et al, 2008; Refuge, no date). The development of trusting relationships is regarded as a prerequisite to exploring sensitive relationship issues with young people (Barter, 2016). Dewar (2015) reports that a peer-led approach to healthy relationship education should not be undervalued, as it encourages a 'safe' environment for discussion by drawing upon the skills of young people as a key resource. The use of peer mentors/educators in schools can result in positive outcomes for young people (McLeod, Jones and Cramer, 2015). However, peer-based programmes need to be appropriately planned, as there is evidence that peer relationships limit the opportunities and willingness to seek support, as support accessed from peers is often inappropriate due to views expressed on the acceptability of abuse/violence (Burton and Kitzinger, 1998; Burman and Cartmel, 2005; Barter et al, 2009). However, as mentioned later, the design and delivery of peer-led interventions needs to ensure that young people are suitably trained, due to the concerns of peer pressure and bullying, but if delivered effectively, they can work to foster an ethos that challenges peer isolation.

The survey conducted for this study indicates that 17 per cent of the participants would access support from their friends. Jennifer felt that she would ask her friends for advice and support:

Interviewer:	If you were wanting some advice on relationships or wanting some support if you didn't feel OK about anything, who would you go to? You've mentioned your sister.
Jennifer:	My friends first, probably, because I'm with them all the time and I text them quite often, so I'd just ask them first.
Interviewer:	Do you think that there's anything that the school can offer then? Teaching, lessons, any information?
Jennifer:	Yeah, give more lessons on how to have a happy relationship and stuff, because they don't really offer much, other than getting people in to come and talk to us. They don't give it as a class.

The regular contact with friends and peers make them an attractive option as a source of advice. The addition of a peer mentoring programme to the repertoire of prevention-based programmes would ensure that young people can appropriately support and guide each other. However, several of the young women interviewed demonstrated the other side of this perspective, that peer relations can also function as a barrier to accessing advice and support. Young women noted that they would often be unwilling to discuss in detail confidential sexual concerns and questions, as a result of the pressure felt from the wider peer group. Therefore, peer groups and "image" were regarded as a "chain" (Glain), which perpetuated the hidden aspect of pressure and concerns within relationships. While young men engaged in sexual banter, the young women described how they discussed their sexual relationships within a different context, primarily a confidential, trusting and serious peer forum. Classroom discussions reinforced peer pressure and the normative expectations of particular behaviour patterns. For example, the expectation was to be in a relationship or sexually active, with the social exclusion from conversations, social media and social gatherings the consequence of diverging from this expected behaviour norm.

The findings from this research demonstrated both the promise and limitations of peer relationships in offering support and relationship guidance to each other. Peer relationships were described as both enabling and disabling as a source of support. Prevention education needs to focus on promoting an ethos of advice/guidance/support rather than judgement and 'peer pressure'. The emphasis needs to be on acceptance, rather than judgement, in order to tackle the concern demonstrated by several young women of the risk of peer isolation as a result of an abusive relationship. The influence of peer relationships observed as critical in shaping heteronormative behaviour patterns, including the pressures on young men and women to conform to a particular gender role, were observed throughout the interviews. Several participants described the pressure on young men to overtly illustrate their sexuality and desires and perform the normative masculine role. Young men were often described as amending their behaviour performance in front of their peers to either "pwdu/sulk" or "dangos ei hun/show off", illustrating the peer pressure on them to conform to normative standards of expected 'laddish' behaviour. Both these behaviour traits shaped whether young men were willing to share the existence of their relationships, that is, the pressure of whether to disclose or hide their relationships, while sexual bravado was described as part of normative banter in the classroom. Several of the young women described the general behaviour of young men of openly discussing sex and rating young women's appearances in the classroom. This often made the young women feel uncomfortable and vulnerable, in particular, as this behaviour was often left unchallenged by their peers. While this indicates that peer support should be viewed with caution, young people access support from each other and should be supported and trained to provide suitable, safe and age-appropriate advice and support to each other.

Participants demonstrated their lack of understanding of the nature of relationships; in particular, they focused on the expected progression of their intimate relationships and their power to be able to select when to have sex and when to 'take a step back' if they did not wish to continue to have sex on a regular basis. Not only was there evidence of the overwhelming pressures and urgency to have sex but also the lack of understanding of sex and relationships. The urgency to discuss sex illustrated the lack of a confidential 'sounding board' with whom to discuss their questions and fears in an autonomous manner within a 'safe space', which was evident as a theme across the interviews. A question several of the young women asked me was whether, once they had started to have sex in a relationship, they then always have to have sex? Despite the value of peer support, several participants said that the requisite support from peer networks felt unsuitable to tackle some of the more complex issues around relationship progression. Intimate relationships were often discussed in detail with peers during a drunken night out, rather than within confidential or everyday relationships.

There was a general lack of confidence in, or indeed willingness to have, in-depth conversations around sex, relationships or any concerns around abuse. As described, "Sometimes I want more, but he's made it clear that he doesn't want more. He decides what we do. My friends don't know" (Glesni). Glesni, who was 18 years old, had a casual relationship with an older male who phoned her to come to his house for sex when he felt like it. She described her feelings about the relationship and indicated that she was too ashamed to discuss the casual nature of their sexual relationship with her friends. Her shame stemmed from the fact that she had previously been "seeing him" but he had later made the decision to bring their relationship to an end and only contacted her on an ad hoc basis to have casual sex. She had told her friends that she wanted a relationship with him and felt that she would be judged for continuing to see him on a casual basis as he had essentially rejected her as a girlfriend.

Peer relationships were described as both enabling and disabling as a source of support by the participants interviewed. There is scant research available on the benefit of peer-facilitated prevention interventions; however, the available evidence does suggest that peer-facilitated education can be effective in shifting young people's attitudes about healthy relationships.

Healthy relationship education: a whole-community approach

Current resources available to tackle the continuum of GBV that includes issues such as abuse in young people's intimate relationships, sexual bullying in schools, 'sexting' and child exploitation are very limited. These harmful issues require a multi-agency, targeted and age-appropriate approach that enables practitioners to respond proactively at a strategic and operational level. While the inclusion of parents/carers as part of any prevention programme is crucial, engagement with young people should be in schools, as this is their primary site of negotiating relationships and their sexuality. Schools are the ideal place for shaping and deterring potential harmful behaviour on a universal platform. In order to ensure that young people receive an independent 'sounding board' and a confidential site in which to discuss their views, any prevention education should be independently facilitated.

The findings discussed here suggest that the key issues are heavily shaped by gender expectations, and therefore should be explicitly discussed with young people, focusing on a range of well-being issues from healthy relationships, equality, respect, consent and intimacy to inappropriate touching, with the aim of protecting them and preventing harm. At the core of prevention work with young people should be a focus on the transformation of unequal power relationships. This research also identified the need to incorporate key discussions on the gendered nature of relationships, and the association of masculinity with power and privilege. Consideration also needs to be given to same-sex relationships and some of the similar, but also different, challenges presented. While this research focused on facilitating a young women-only space in which to discuss their attitudes towards and experiences of intimate relationships, research in the future requires attention on the pressures imposed on young men.

The ethos of working towards a 'whole-system' approach to addressing GBV has been discussed on an international and national platform. On a global platform, the Istanbul Convention outlines the requirement to establish and deliver services based on a coordinated and holistic approach to financing and service implementation. Key guidance has focused on introducing arrangements for developing multi-agency services to address domestic abuse (NICE, 2016), with four 'pillars' to ending violence against women and girls being established: prevention, provision of services, partnership working and pursuing perpetrators (HM Government, 2016). There is also an expectation for local areas to develop a collaborative, robust and effective response to ending violence against women and girls through strategic principles that establish a whole-system approach (Home Office, 2016). The potential impact of a whole-system, holistic or integrated approach has a wider reach in comparison with individualised approaches to violence prevention (Cordis Bright, 2019).

Nelson and Baldwin (2016) caution against the overuse of an individualised approach when working to address child protection issues, specifically, sexual abuse, as not getting to the root cause of the issue. Abusive behaviour fosters a culture of isolation, shame and stigma that functions as a barrier to reporting concerns and experiences of abuse. This sense of isolation, shame and stigma is often supported by a culture of reprisal across young people's wider community and peer group, including the harmful impact of gossip and rumours, which can ultimately 'spoil' a young woman's identity. The process of 'giving voice' needs to have a 'real-world' approach that acknowledges and addresses the realities of poverty, discrimination and inequalities, and be focused on promoting positive empowerment and well-being. While individualised support is required, the overall aim of prevention and early interventions needs to be strategic and systematic.

As such, there is a need for a whole-community approach, with a core aim of tackling the harmful attitudes that scaffold this form of abuse and the perpetration of abuse, as both a social problem and a well-being issue. This idea of a 'whole-community approach' is based on the principles of an ecological model. The ecological framework was original devised by Bronfenbrenner (1979), focusing on the relationships and interchanges between all variables of the model across the micro, meso, exo, macro and chronosystems. Ecological models concentrate on attitudes and beliefs (individual), family and peers (relationships), cultural social norms (community) and policies and rule of law (societal). Therefore, the aim is to connect this social problem with the individual and wider community structural factors, in order to interconnect both layers to assist in shaping a 'whole' or comprehensive response to the problem. This model, while focusing on interconnected factors, places the individual at the core of the issue, bringing a rich attention to individual experiences over time (the chronosystem), therefore 'working with' young people, multi-agency stakeholders and the wider community to give voice to and empower each layer of the system by building on strengths and assets. This will encourage an approach focused on universal preventions across the community to address social norms and attitudes, in partnership with another layer of interventions concentrated on bespoke individualised support based on assessed needs. The nature of the problem of GBV towards young women is complex and involves multiple causes of individual, social and cultural factors that need an intersectoral approach in order to tackle it. This model aims to deconstruct the current historical patterns of gendered social norms by working across each layer of the system.

Having a community-focused model to address abuse in young intimate relationships not only aligns with models suggested to address child sexual abuse (Nelson and Baldwin, 2016), through work with wider communities to address child sexual exploitation (Public Health England, 2019) and wider community engagement to end youth gang violence (Home Office, 2015), but it also blends with the approaches of planning and developing services based on current and future population needs. The whole-community approach focuses on addressing the root cause of abuse in young people's intimate relationships, and the impact of harmful gendered social norms across local communities, by adopting a culture of cooperation, multi-agency working and effective communication in order to evaluate and address this social problem in a bespoke manner across diverse communities. As previously discussed, abuse in young people's intimate relationships is much more visible than adult domestic abuse, allowing a better platform to address this social problem as a whole-community issue. The core aims of any preventative programme should focus on:

- promoting communities focused on challenging attitudes that support structural inequalities that favour men and young men;
- raising awareness of the nature and impact of this form of abuse;
- increasing the safety of those experiencing this form of abuse;
- reducing the stigma and shame associated with this form of abuse;
- adopting a multi-agency and clear pathway for screening, assessing and addressing this issue;
- offering a bespoke, person-centred and flexible model of interventions that is adaptable to individual needs;
- offering a model of support that is focused on support, active listening and understanding;

- offering a model that is focused on promoting positive empowerment and well-being.

The development of a whole-community approach is informed by a robust and inclusive co-productive and partnership approach which considers the structural, community and individual level factors that influence the nature and prevalence of this form of abuse. At the foundation of this approach is a core community of practice (CoP) that shapes the development of the approach in a bespoke and targeted manner based on the population needs analysis of the community in question. Therefore, there are two key elements that formulate the foundation of this whole-community approach: firstly, the multi-agency CoP, and, secondly, the completion of a local population needs assessment.

A CoP can be defined as a community that shares a practice to address a joint issue, through regular communication, focused on knowledge development and reflective practice (Hoadley, 2012; Ng and Pemberton, 2013; Bond-Taylor and Davies, 2020). Within this model, the aim of the CoP is to provide strategic and practical direction to the development of a multi-agency approach in order to address this social problem. The aim of a population needs assessment within this context is to gather all the available multi-disciplinary data in order to understand the nature of this problem, specifically, in the context of the local population in order to understand the needs of the community. A needs assessment should essentially focus on outlining data on the level of need regarding this specific issue, the extent of unmet need, the pattern of supply and effectiveness of current services and how to use resources in the most effective and efficient way. The process could primarily follow an epidemiological approach, mainly based on gathering quantitative data to estimate the size and composition of the population of interest, including information of time and prevalence rates and the current provision of services to meet those needs. There could also be an element of a comparative approach, to focus on establishing a data comparison of this issue across specific areas within this community. The methodology could also concentrate on gathering the 'lived experiences', stories and qualitative information directly from young people and stakeholders to explore current needs and priorities for future provision. The work programme established by the CoP should be monitored and reviewed on a quarterly basis. As part of this process, there should be a community mapping exercise exploring:

- existing policies, procedures, services and interventions focused on addressing this issue (on a universal and individual level with survivors and perpetrators), with data available illustrating the context and nature of the problem, staff on a multi-agency basis who are trained champions, awareness and specialist training;

- undertaking a multi-agency local population needs analysis to target the whole-community approach in a bespoke manner to the needs of the local community – that is, having a sense of where the resources and interventions should be targeted, for example, young men in male-dominated environments, in order to develop a mindset of a safer and equal community.

Table 6.1 outlines what the focus should essentially be on.

The objective is that this level of understanding assists in the planning of service delivery on a multi-agency basis, including the prioritising of the allocation of resources to meet the identified needs based on local data. On

Table 6.1: Foundation of whole-community approach

Recommendation	Action
Identifying the nature of the issue	The focus of the population needs assessment is on identifying multi-disciplinary data outlining the nature of abuse as part of young people's intimate relationships.
Identifying the population	Mapping the data and needs of all young people aged 12–18 years old within this local community, with specific emphasis on the continuum of abusive behaviour within young intimate relationships. This will provide a clear sense of the size, profile and demographics of this particular group (in order to develop a demographic profile of the population of interest: age, gender, geographic location, urban–rural location, household composition, disability, ethnic group and so on).
Identifying data sources	Undertaking a mapping exercise of the profile of all key agencies within the community that works with young people aged 12–18. This could essentially be focused on creating a community profile of young people-focused services as key stakeholders. Other stakeholders may also include relevant sectors that may be able to provide data/information and work to address this issue, for example, stakeholders or businesses within the night-time economy, such as fast-food establishments, nightclubs, taxi companies and so on.
Identifying the gap between needs and services	Analysing the data as part of the workstream of the CoP to outline an overview and a workplan focused on addressing the gap between demand and supply. This will outline a sense of the profile of services available and the effectiveness and cost-effectiveness of these services in meeting the current and future projected needs of this population group. This could shape the policy framework and the requirement of the stakeholders around service design and resource allocation (including an idea of best value and cost-effective solutions). There is also a requirement of highlighting and understanding the strengths and weaknesses of data sources as well as analytic skills.
Involving young people	Including young people as key members of the CoP, to give them voice, choice and control in order to inform the gathering, analysis and application of the data to inform the community work plan. This will also inform the design of services based on the views of young people as the population of interest.

a strategic level, this workstream can inform the development of services and the commissioning framework required to shape current and future service delivery. This level of data analysis offers the opportunity to implement a universal intervention programme and a targeted, individualised approach. For example, the universal approach will include a focus on raising awareness and understanding, while a targeted approach could include individual interventions to address the impact of abuse experiences as part of an intimate relationship. The foundation of universal and targeted interventions will be based on the understanding that abuse in young intimate relationships is as a result of power, control and unequal social relations.

As part of this work, the shape of the multi-agency strategy outlines the community-focused key objectives, outcomes and measures. This model focuses on the solution at all levels of the community, with attention on a bespoke preventative approach which is owned across the multi-agency CoP. Not only will this foster a culture of a whole-community approach but it will also include key agency partners who would not otherwise recognise or acknowledge their role in preventing abuse in young intimate relationships and create an effective working environment through a shared vision of key principles.

Key principles of a whole-community approach

The aim of a whole-community approach is to empower a sense of community partnership based on a shared vision and agreed goals focused on working towards shared principles.

Having a focus on a whole-community approach to preventing abuse in young intimate relationships will ensure that the attention is on social integration, community cohesion and established core values based on shared accountability. Table 6.2 outlines the key principles of a whole community approach. Table 6.3 outlines the membership for a whole community approach.

Whole-community approach toolkit

A specialist- and practitioner-focused toolkit would be useful in outlining a comprehensive approach to addressing this issue, outlining the context of the issue, the referral pathway, the screening tool, the assessment tool and the intervention programme that can be adapted to be used on a one-to-one or group basis with young people. This is a collaborative tool, allowing workers on a multi-agency basis to have a conversation with young people in a compassionate and safe manner. The toolkit will include practitioner checklists, a risk and well-being screening tool, a well-being assessment tool (including guidance on assessing and scoring each assessment domain), a safety planning checklist and a comprehensive interventions programme.

Table 6.2: Key principles of a whole-community approach

Key principle	Description
Define, name and conceptualise the whole-community approach	Outlining the conceptual framework should consider the findings from this research and focus on a gendered approach to this form of abuse. This focus should endeavour to include young men as part of the solution in a proactive manner. Care should also be taken regarding labelling young men as offenders or perpetrators. It's also important to decide whether young women experiencing this form of abuse are defined as victims or survivors. There should also be a focus on intersectional needs, identity and well-being when defining this issue, concentrated on an intersectional approach to understanding the cultural context and experiences of individual young women. An intersectional frame to the programme will ensure that the broad range of intersecting needs informing young people's identities can inform the foundation for the risk, vulnerability and well-being factors that require assessment. It is important to align the agreed definition with the Istanbul Convention and the Domestic Abuse Act 2021. This approach should focus on establishing an intersectional practice model which offers accessible services to young people who identify as BME, disabled, LGBTQQI and those from isolated or marginalised communities (urban and rural). The emphasis should be on reducing barriers around access to services when working with young people with multiple needs, rather than labelling them as having 'complex needs' or being 'hard to reach'. The work of the CoP and the community needs to be flexible and responsive to changing needs and diverse identities across the community, which means empowering all to access services.
Changing community norms: focused on challenging normative attitudes	Focused on an understanding of abuse as a result of unequal power relations due to harmful gendered social norms and structural inequalities. There was a sense that young men's abusive behaviour was natural, and was justified as a response to provocation by their girlfriends. This raises two key points for the design of prevention education. Firstly, there is a need to challenge our understanding of young men and men's behaviour, gendered norms of femininity, masculinity, abuse, violence and aggression. Young people should receive education and support through the adoption of a gender lens, in order to understand how they use gender to naturalise, justify and excuse abusive behaviour. Secondly, there is a need to have institutional responses concentrated on shaping youth mainstream cultures of gendered norms, rather than individualistic notions of justifiable or expected behaviour. Changing attitudes towards a continuum of abuse in young relationships.
Preventing abuse within young intimate relationships	Changing the attitudes of the whole community towards the gendered nature of abuse within young intimate relationships and the influence of harmful gendered social norms. Abusive behaviour in teenage relationships was overtly displayed in schools, indicating a lack of awareness of acceptable behaviours or the need to hide this harmful display. This reflects that it has become acceptable among young people to display these types of behaviour in the public arena, reflecting their normalisation of verbal and emotional abuse. The visibility of this behaviour may not necessarily function as a protective factor, and requires specific consideration when designing prevention programmes. As part of this work, a focus should be on removing the barriers to accessing support, reducing shame and stigma as a result of experiencing abuse and tackling social isolation for those who experience abuse.

Table 6.2: Key principles of a whole-community approach (continued)

Key principle	Description
	Current conversations on prevention focus on the avoidance of risk, rather than pleasure and healthy relationships. Prevention education needs to have a greater focus on developing spaces to enable young women to develop their own sexual identities, including a re-focus on sexual desire, pleasure and love.
Co-production: voice, choice and control	Valuing the voice, choice and control of young people. Creating a culture and ethos informed by everyday experiences as the approach is focused on giving young people a voice and the power to be active participants in the CoP. Young women have shared the view that they want interventions that empower them to make informed choices by giving them the scripts to reject unwanted attention/requests, as they wanted to learn about "how to say 'no' to guys, no to sex, no to pictures" (Aleysha) and "need to know about respect and keeping sex lives private" (Claire). There was a sense from participants that there is sufficient information available on how and where to get support. Despite this, there was criticism that the support was not specialist or targeted to address their concerns, as the focus was primarily on the biological aspects of sex, rather than the emotional aspects of intimate relationships. There was also a call to focus the delivery of any preventative session on practical matters, such as relationship coping strategies and supporting young people to conceptualise what was 'normal', expected or simply 'OK' in relationships.
Empowering the community	Offers a systems-wide, integrated approach across the community aligned with the key principles of the Istanbul Convention. Empowers the community as a whole to change the local landscape and to identify and address abuse in young intimate relationships.
Partnership working arrangements	Creating a sense of community ownership to change the acceptability and nature of this form of abuse focused on fostering community connectedness through a CoP. Formulating a foundation of change based on a partnership between a professional and the wider community to design, develop and deliver bespoke approaches as solutions to prevent this form of abuse.
Evidence-based	Evidence based on a detailed population needs assessment of the community in question. The assessment is to include analysis of multi-agency data, including a focus on the community capabilities, including looking at strengths, and protective and risk factors.
Promoting safety	The approach will promote safety by providing all staff members at every level with the knowledge and skills to identify the signs and symptoms of abuse, including a focus on training staff to follow appropriate steps to respond to disclosure. Having a core focus on safeguarding and safety planning to ensure that survivors are safe at every point. Designing and implementing a whole-community approach toolkit, which outlines a whole-systems approach to practically addressing this issue at both universal and individual level. Offering robust protection and safety planning for those young women experiencing abuse within their intimate relationships. Offering a private space for young people to disclose abuse experience and to discuss any questions or concerns they wish to raise.

(continued)

Table 6.2: Key principles of a whole-community approach (continued)

Key principle	Description
Focused on promoting positive well-being	Offering support in a manner that detects the problem, and responding with consideration to individual needs and well-being to reduce the short- and long-term impact of abuse. Well-being: there were several barriers and enablers for young women when attempting to access support provision. The importance of privacy was crucial, as several young women noted that queuing for an appointment with the school nurse only served to raise questions and gossip (primarily around sex, in particular, contraception and unwanted pregnancies). The status of the professional was also important, as there was a general consensus that they would not access the school child protection lead, as this was often the deputy head. This was primarily due to their fear that the information would be shared and dealt with disproportionately, and due to their perception that this role was disengaged from them as students.

Table 6.3: Potential key members of a whole-community approach

Key members	Description
Based on a multi-agency CoP, including key stakeholders from the community and young people	The key roles and responsibilities of the 'whole-community' group should be outlined within the agreed terms of reference.
Ownership by key leaders on a multi-agency basis	Designing a whole-community approach local strategic plan to outline the direction of local multi-agency commissioning and funding arrangements.
Establishing multi-agency and community specialists	Training a group of champions across key agencies to be able to deliver awareness training on abuse in young people's intimate relationships. The group of specialist champions to also be trained to be able to respond to disclosures of abuse.
Promoting the voices of young people	Commission a young person-focused service to provide advocacy, support and interventions to different groups of young people in a bespoke manner to address this issue.

Assessment

Before discussing the design and delivery of prevention interventions, it is important to discuss the assessment tool used to assess the risk of domestic abuse. Any assessment tool used with young people should be implemented as part of a person–centred conversation focused on their overall well-being. When professionals have concerns about relationship abuse and violence, consideration should be given to the appropriate use of the young people's 'DASH' risk identification checklist (SafeLives, 2014) to assist in completing a holistic assessment of need and risk, or the Duluth Teen Power and Control

Wheel, to start the conversation about healthy relationships with young people. However, based on the findings of this research, I would suggest some changes to the 'DASH' checklist for young people, including:

- The tool needs to focus on the fluid and less established nature of young people's relationships.
- The first question of the tool asks the young person 'Are you frightened?' The focus should be on exploring with the young person the context of his/her relationship.
- The tool asks the young person whether they would involve the police. While it is important to ask this question, there needs to be a broader focus on whether the young person would involve a professional agency, and whether they have a sympathetic individual that they can talk to and gain support from.
- The assessment asks if the young person is pregnant. However, it should firstly ask about the status of their relationship, and more about the nature of their sexual contact, with more of a focus on sexual coercion and consent.
- The tool focuses heavily on physical abuse and needs to look at the continuum of abusive behaviour.

Recommendations for programme design in schools

To complement the whole-community approach, a healthy relationship education in schools should focus on supporting young people to address their needs on an everyday basis. The themes from this research suggested that the design and delivery of prevention education should consider the following:

- Currently, the role of young people in shaping their learning content and delivery of healthy relationships is limited. This study illustrates the benefit of gaining young people's input and advice on matters that affect them. Aligned with Article 12 of the UNCRC, young people should be provided with the space to participate and assist key professionals to design the content and delivery of prevention programmes. Schools should also engage with parents and carers, and the wider community, on this topic.
- As indicated by the findings here, it is well established that attitudes supportive of unequal gender roles and abusive behaviour are predictors of the tolerance of abuse in young intimate relationships. There was a sense from the young women that young men's abusive behaviour was natural and justified as a response to provocation by their girlfriends ("I was a typical girl" [Aleysha]). This raises three key points for the design of prevention education. Firstly, there is a need to challenge our

understanding of young men's and men's behaviour, and the gendered norms of femininity, masculinity, abuse, violence and aggression ("he did the typical angry boy thing" [Aleysha]). Secondly, professionals should be mindful of the current levels of young women's empowerment and challenge the belief that, within a post-feminist discourse, young women have powerful relational positions. Thirdly, there is a need to have an institutional response focused on shaping youth mainstream cultures of gendered norms, rather than individualistic notions of justifiable or expected behaviour. Not only will this address the foundation of gendered expectations, inequality and sexism but it will also empower key agencies in youth and education settings to deliver education which will reshape youth identities.

- Limited prevention interventions exist to systematically address the broad range of GBV as a continuum of harm and to make connections between individual acts of abuse, broader cultural norms and structural power inequalities. As a key aspect of any prevention education, there needs to be an outline of the signs and symptoms of abuse in intimate relationships, including exploration of the continuum of abusive behaviour, coercive control and incorporating the role of digital technologies to take account of young people's realities. There was a general suggestion by the young women participating in this research that there should be several focused tutorial sessions on the meaning(s) of a 'healthy relationship'. Programmes should include practical learning around being in intimate relationships, and the expectations and boundaries within these relationships. This call for a practical understanding is aligned with the view of the young women interviewed that practical 'life lessons' should be included as part of PSHE.

- Evidence from this present research highlights the need to address sexual double standards, in particular, regarding the sexualisation of young women and the non-consensual circulation of images. The use of the new media technologies and sexting should be a key aspect of prevention education in order to ensure that the heteronormative expectations reinforcing sexual double standards, and the inception of a 'laddish culture', are confronted. Not only does this perpetuate the harm experienced by young women, but it also reinforces the peer pressures and expectations on young men to conform to 'laddish expectations'.

- A key theme from the interview narratives was the growing dominance of social media, the visibility of porn, the everyday application of coercive sexting behaviour and the routine requests for 'nudie' photos, which suggests a need to drive forward robust prevention education in order to tackle these harmful attitudes and behaviours. Sexting has the potential to replicate sexist and gendered attitudes, in particular, coercive behaviour and the objectification of women. Healthy relationship education should target the promotion of a balanced consideration of sexting, pornography, consent and sexual double standards, including the potential negative impact on their well-being.

- 'Healthy relationship' education should avoid the use of stereotypes that reinforce the ethos of victim blaming, for example, the findings from this research that young women were advised by the police to monitor their behaviour and dress sense on a night out. The focus should be on involving young people in education on the engagement of sexuality in a gendered and unequal society.
- Current conversations on prevention focus on the avoidance of risk, rather than pleasure and healthy relationships. Prevention education needs to have a greater emphasis on talking about the emotional aspects of intimate relationships, including love.
- There was also a sense that young women wanted prevention interventions that practically empowered them to make informed choices and gave them the scripts to reject unwanted attention/requests, as they wanted to learn about "How to say 'no' to guys, no to sex, no to pictures" (Aleysha) and "Need to know about respect and keeping sex lives private" (Claire).

Programme delivery

- Schools should be the main site for delivering prevention education on 'healthy relationships', as over 90 per cent of the young women surveyed subscribed to the idea that schools should work to prevent and address sexual harassment and bullying.
- A general consensus was that receiving sex education in year 8 was 'out of context' as it did not feel relevant, with the young women stating that sex education should focus on a broader curriculum focused on the experiences of being in intimate relationships as a whole. There was a feeling that receiving isolated sessions on sex education in year 8 was insufficient, as it purely explored the mechanics of having sex, rather than the nature of intimate relationships. There was a sense that relationship education should commence in year 8, especially as several of the young women in years 12 and 13 noted that they lacked the understanding and confidence to explore aspects of relationship norms, etiquette and expected progression. The consequences of not receiving appropriate advice and support were highlighted: "There's not enough sex education or support – girls then harm themselves – some have been in bad relationships and they have no help" (Aleysha).
- Healthy relationship interventions should be separated from interventions addressing risky behaviour. Though this research is based on young women's experiences, and thus reflects the gendered nature and patterns

of harm experienced due to GBV, prevention interventions should be designed to address both young men's and young women's needs, so as to include both as part of this conversation.

- The expertise of professionals working for key agencies, such as the police, social care, education, youth services and the voluntary sector, will be vital to the success and effective impact of any prevention/early intervention activities adopted with young people. There were suggestions around training and supervision offered to practitioners when working to support young people in dealing with the plethora of issues surrounding young intimate relationships.

The use of media/films to highlight key messages about abuse in intimate relationships was also suggested as a form of prevention education, in particular, as the impact of the televised BBC film *Murdered by my Boyfriend* (2014)[5] was reinforced during several of the interviews. As previously mentioned, the use of media/films as part of a prevention campaign should be incorporated as one of a broader range of programmes, rather than used as a stand-alone prevention intervention in order to avoid the potential for the 'boomerang effect' and the contradictory identifications with both anti-violence messages and victim-blaming discourses. From the interviews, the impact of viewing this film was evident:

Interviewer:	What would help young people?
Ceri:	Maybe it's a stupid idea, but a TV programme. There was one on an abusive relationship, everyone was talking about it, so it's showed that young people watch that kind of stuff and that it can help young people learn for themselves what's OK and not OK in a relationship.
Interviewer:	Do you know what the show was called?
Ceri:	*Abused by my Boyfriend.*
Interviewer:	Do you mean *Murdered by my Boyfriend*?
Ceri:	Yes, that's it – it was on the BBC and it was a true story. You just felt so sorry for her – it was so shocking.
Interviewer:	Did it make a difference that it was a true story?
Ceri:	Yes, it brought it back to reality.
Interviewer:	Did anything in particular shock you?
Ceri:	Yes, the fact that he was taking her money, I just thought *wow*, that's out of order, and all the bruises and the ending, *wow*, that actually happened.

Ceri discusses how the film was "shocking" and had resulted in "everyone talking about it". She also highlights how this type of film can give young people messages about 'healthy relationships' and the continuum of abusive and violent behaviour on an everyday basis.

- Several young women noted the benefit of research and their involvement in this project as a space in which to discuss their attitudes and experiences. The development of interventions should be completed in partnership with young people in order to ensure the inclusion of their voice and to empower them to take control of their own lives. Young people are more likely to be engaged in whatever choices they make, and have better outcomes, if they are involved throughout the process.
- Linked to the messages from the young women's narratives of observing abuse within relationships (for example, Glain and Mair), prevention education should also have a focus on the bystander perspective in order to empower young people and teaching staff to safely challenge inappropriate behaviour when it occurs.

Active empowerment and reshaping gendered social norms

This book has explored the impact of gendered expectations on young women's abilities to navigate the 'uncharted territory' of young intimate relationships. The intention was not to establish prevalence rates of abuse but rather to propose a fresh perspective on young intimate relationships by promoting young women as active agents. The young women's narratives illustrated the challenge of shifting young men's power, due to the cultural attitudes that perpetuate established hierarchical gendered identities which favour men over women.

Young women continue to face challenges when negotiating their feminine identity, in particular, sexual 'double standards'. The presence and harmful impact of patterns of harassment, emotional abuse and coercive control experienced on an 'everyday' basis were evident across all the discussions with the young women. The role of gender norms in shaping their relationship scripts, including their views on abuse and violence, was evident. Despite their ability to share attitudes focused on gender equality, they demonstrated limited empowerment and space to draw upon this understanding within their intimate relationships. Young women's constructions of their attitudes, identities and relationship experiences suggest a gap between their desires, expectations and actual everyday experiences. As a result, the young women adapted their expectations and repeatedly demonstrated how they restricted their voice, choice and control within their intimate relationships in order to avoid rejection. They adapted their wishes, feelings and expectations and, as a result, remained in unhealthy relationships. As part of this, the majority of the young women, specifically those who had experiences of intimate relationships, continued to demonstrate attitudes supportive of gender equality, reflecting both their limited power to change their reality and influence established gender norms on their own relationship experiences. The young women performed what they saw as the expected girlfriend role to satisfy the needs of their audience, essentially, to maintain what Goffman termed as 'facework' (Goffman, 1955), paying 'lip service' to their boyfriends' demands to the detriment of their own self-development of identity.

Attitudes, gender norms and abuse

The everyday 'doing of' gender both reflects and influences young people's role and power within their intimate relationships. Young women naturalised and justified the nature and patterns of abusive behaviour experienced. As a result, the young women's power to negotiate their identity and experiences within their intimate relationships is limited, and often results in their emotion work to mask their genuine wishes and feelings. The voices of the young women interviewed illustrate the influence of the harmful social interactions experienced both within their everyday schooling and their relationship experiences as the 'norm', rather than problematic behaviour. Due to the gendered structural power hierarchy, the young women lacked the power or space to challenge these norms, and therefore the behaviour was accepted and often left unchallenged. As discussed, they clearly demonstrated attitudes that reflect the awareness and understanding of gender equality and healthy relationships; however, the dynamics within their own intimate relationships remained problematic. This influenced the performance of their role within their relationships, which was passive and reactive to the behaviour of their boyfriend.

Understanding the nature of the relationship between pro-abuse attitudes and abusive behaviour will enable us to gauge whether attitudes reflect the idea of abusive behaviour on a continuum of interlinked 'everyday experiences'. If we are to understand the nature and patterns of abuse in teenage relationships, then we must understand how young people construct meaning(s) about their gender, their sexual selves, their relationship aspirations and their understanding of attitudes towards 'good' and 'bad' relationships. Creating the space for a 'women-only' questionnaire on attitudes towards young intimate relationships provided an overall sense of a shift away from the ethos of attitudes which are accepting of particular violence and abuse in specific circumstances.

The young women's general attitudes and beliefs towards gendered norms reflected a rejection of essentialism, and the ideology of the breadwinning male and housewife. It was identified that the young women were able to articulate 'healthy' relationship attitudes, both with reference to equal gender roles and their views on the role of young women within intimate relationships. Overall, the attitudes of participants questioned the acceptability of abuse within heterosexual and same-sex relationships. The attitudes identified in the survey findings were focused on an ideology of equality, whereas their intimate relationship experiences evident in the interviews generally revealed their limited and unequal power base. This indicates the challenges where narratives about equalisation and aspirations are far removed from expectations, and their perceived and real positions in intimate relationships. Moreover, this position was further exacerbated by their lack of tools with which to address these inequalities or negotiate any degree of power within relationships within a period where there was a presumption of equality.

There was a general resistance to, and justification of, somewhat subtle forms of coercion, harassment and control. The extent of acceptability was shaped by their image of traditional gendered norms and expectations. In many instances, the young women failed to propose an alternative script to the hegemonic masculinity they were experiencing within their own intimate relationship. The popular narratives of men's "nature", "that's how they are" and "I'm just a 'psycho bitch'" (Aleysha) were reinforced when prioritising what young men wanted from relationships, primarily as a result of the fear of rejection. Not only did this reinforce the perspective that male demands and desires were prioritised but also that the notion of casual sex was accepted, as men were seen as naturally commitment-phobic. This sense of symbolic gendering (Lamont, 2014), basically the norm or cultural feature of courtship, revealed the perceived benefits and comfort gained from accepting established gendered scripts, rather than suffering the consequences of non-conformity. Thus, it was permitted and expected for young men to have a focus on the physicality of intimate relationships, while young women were expected to lack desire and be passive. The young women described how they were constantly on the receiving end of 'sexual double standards', where all options open to them would leave them open to the judgement of others. The ingrained fear of transgressing gender norms and challenging this sexual emphasis placed them within the quandary of having 'sexual double standards'.

Young women's experiences demonstrated that the presence of traditional gendered norms favouring young men was damaging for them in their intimate relationships in three distinct ways: firstly, due to the construction of the young women's propensity to be 'emotional' as a justification for controlling and abusive behaviour; secondly, due to their perceived sexual weakness in contrast to male dominance and desire; and, thirdly, on account of the naturalisation of emotional, abusive and coercive behaviour. The participants justified abusive behaviour in their 'passive' role of being 'reactive' to the 'moods' of their boyfriends under the pressure of conforming to the ideal girlfriend role. It was apparent that young women lacked the power to operationalise their egalitarian attitudes in order to engage in relationships that adhere to the description of what they expect, want or desire within a 'healthy relationship'. As a default position, they relied and drew upon normative scripts focused on essentialist beliefs. This research reflected the complex emotion work that emerged in young women's narratives of intimate relationships. The young women undertook the daily 'impression management' of performing both the 'doing of gender' and their perceived 'ideal girlfriend' role, often to their own detriment. The young women demonstrated how they carefully managed their 'performance of self' and the management of their own identity (Goffman, 1963).

Therefore, their claim of gender equality does not translate into their everyday relationships, further concealing and reinforcing their lack of power, negotiation and choice when performing their role within intimate relationships. This book supports and contributes to the understanding that young women are limited in their capacity to challenge established gender norms that restrict their sexual identities and performance of self. It can be argued that barriers preventing the operationalisation of their attitudes, beliefs, wishes and feelings reinforced gender differences, providing unstable grounding for a change towards 'real' gender equality. As a result, preparing young men to relinquish at least a portion of their power needs to be incorporated as part of prevention education. Based on the benefits observed from conducting this research within a space specifically open to young women, particularly the engagement of them in the advisory group stage, there are potential benefits of delivering a combination of single- and mixed-gender prevention interventions.

Gender norms, social media and online abuse

Throughout the discussion with young women, the importance of social media was evident across this age group, with over 90 per cent surveyed owning a mobile phone with internet access, 83.3 per cent accessing Facebook and 75 per cent using Snapchat. The findings from the questionnaire revealed attitudes rejecting the view that girlfriends should be constantly available 'online' to respond to their boyfriends. The experiences shared by the young women illustrated the full complexity of this 'online' behaviour, which was described in contradictory terms by participants as desired, unwanted, coercive, sexual and accidental. There was a degree of confusion of identifying 'online' behaviour as abusive, as some of the attitudes were accepting of behaviour that does not explicitly appear to be verbally or physically abusive. This confusion also extended to their attitudes towards online 'lad culture', specifically, their degree of ambivalence between their role and the pressure of the system of appearance 'rating' as a popularity currency.

The young women revealed the automatic entitlement of young men to attend parties and social gatherings, and maintain a much more explicit online presence on social media sites. Within established older relationships, it was used as a coercive tool in order to monitor virtual relationships and check online behaviour, for example, the 'likes' on Facebook pictures, the change in Facebook relationship status and the practice by young people of 'blocking' individuals from their girlfriend's/boyfriend's page. There was a general view that if you were in a relationship, you had to modify your behaviour, in particular, if you were in a photo and it was posted on Facebook. However, the young women's reactions to these photos/selfies were described as different from their boyfriends', with their overall tendency not to react or say anything for fear of triggering an argument or explicitly sharing their jealous feelings, as it was perceived as a sign of insecurity and 'neediness'. These feelings continued to remain hidden as the relationship progressed.

The practice around requesting nudies was also highly gendered and coercive. The experiences described within the qualitative interviews around 'sexting' and 'nudies' were primarily focused on sexual inclusion/exclusion, consent and control. Again, the young women's narratives revealed the confusing and often contradictory challenges faced when negotiating their sexual identities. Not only are there different expectations of behaviour 'online' and 'offline', for example, the dilemma of acting in a passive or 'subtle' manner 'offline' and revealing and sharing 'nudie' photos 'online', but their experiences and power in navigating the often uncharted territory of 'online' intimate relationships was limited, often confusing and unclear.

Well-being, identity and abuse

The consequences of abuse on young women's well-being and identity were discussed throughout. Their experiences of intimate relationships revealed the presence of a range of harmful behaviours when considering the continuum of abusive behaviour (Kelly, 1988). However, not all behaviours were identified as 'harmful' or abusive, which questions their understanding of a healthy relationship. The presence of emotional harm was the most visible behaviour, which underpinned and sustained wider harmful behaviours in all these cases, as well as appearing as a form of isolated harm. This was closely followed by overt verbal abuse, coercive controlling behaviour and online patterns of abuse. This demonstrated the sustained and harmful impact of the new media technologies on young women's well-being when used to perpetuate abuse, control and bullying behaviour within virtual spaces. This coercive controlling behaviour also included sexual coercion and threatening behaviour. However, there were no explicit examples of financial abuse or direct physical harm. These harmful behaviours, in particular, verbal abuse and controlling behaviour, were often played out within the public sphere, within view of, or at least in the knowledge of, their peers and often also their family members. This may be due to the routine of the daily contact of young people within large mixed gender groups within school and other learning environments. This is in sharp contrast to the 'hidden' nature of adult domestic abuse, as it remains a concealed and highly stigmatised issue within more mature relationships. The negative experiences of feeling shame, stigma, sexism and harassment both online and offline were oppressive and visible. While this visibility means that the patterns of abuse in young people's intimate relationships and wider communities are transparent rather than hidden, it also raises the challenge of addressing harmful behaviour that is well known, rehearsed and permitted. This is a key challenge for any prevention interventions with young people.

The experiences of the young women interviewed reflected the impact of these forms of abuse on their overall well-being, both physical and emotional. The harm, upset and impact of the abuse was reflected in the deterioration of their physical and emotional well-being, with the abuse often leading to their isolation from their community as a whole. The impact on their identity was also evident in several ways. Firstly, their lack of power and control to operationalise their attitudes and beliefs of healthy relationships as part of their intimate relationships, and therefore the need to reshape their beliefs in order to have an intimate relationship. Secondly, the requirement for young women to be 'passive', again with regards to sharing their true beliefs but also with regards to their ability to share their desires and sexual identity, specifically due to the oppressive constant presence of gendered 'sexual double standards'. Young women's identities often became 'spoilt' when they acted in a manner that was perceived to be contrary to social norms and the presumed 'natural' sexual passivity in women. The challenge faced by the young women interviewed was negotiating a female identity, with shifting appropriateness of this 'double standard' dictated by the requirement to be virginal, while also being available to sexually please the opposite sex. Due to their lack of power, 'emotion work' was undertaken in order to disguise their true feelings and beliefs of their wishes, desires and their concept of a healthy relationship. They had the knowledge and understanding of the meaning of a healthy relationship, but lacked the power or control to challenge unacceptable or abusive behaviours. Finally, participants described negotiating their identity and the performance of self (Goffman, 1963) within settings and communities which actively restricted their identity, behaviour, physical choice and liberty.

A whole-community approach

The importance of a comprehensive educational approach, focused on understanding and questioning gender norms, promoting gender equality and healthy relationships cannot be ignored. Prevention programmes geared towards empowering young women should focus on promoting their confidence and individual agency. This re-evaluation will assist them to construct their position in a manner that reduces the likelihood that any form of negotiation and power comes at a cost. This cost, seen within their narratives, was the emotion work of the management of this power imbalance and the requirement to 'subtly' perform their expected girlfriend role, due to the lack of negotiating space within their intimate relationships. The gaps between young women's attitudes, their desires, expectations and their 'everyday' experiences draw attention to the complex dilemma for young women when performing their role in intimate relationships.

The development of a policy on 'healthy relationship' education should focus on a 'whole-community approach' that includes a focus on tackling gender norms, stigma and shame as its foundation. The focus of this policy should go beyond the school setting in order to incorporate key multi-agency stakeholders, parents/carers and the wider community as a whole. The ethos of including young people and other key stakeholders to co-produce intervention tools to be used with young people should also be a key component of this policy.

The findings suggest the importance of a comprehensive educational approach, focused on understanding and questioning gender norms, promoting gender equality and healthy relationships. The benefits observed from conducting this research within a space specifically open to young women, particularly the engagement of them in the advisory group stage, suggests the potential advantages of delivering a combination of single- and mixed-gender prevention interventions. To summarise, this study reveals the presence and harmful impact of patterns of harassment experienced by young women on an 'everyday' basis, and the sustained emotional abuse and coercive control experienced by them within their intimate relationships. The young women performed what they saw as the expected girlfriend role to satisfy the needs of their audience, essentially, to maintain what Goffman termed as 'facework' (Goffman, 1955), paying 'lip service' to their boyfriends' demands to the detriment of their own self-development of identity.

The young women were able to demonstrate clear knowledge of the support services available, both on a local and national level. Despite the general willingness of the participants to access support services, barriers to accessing support were identified: firstly, the lack of services to discuss the emotional aspects of intimate relationships; secondly, the shame and stigma of acknowledging being in a 'bad relationship'; thirdly, the need for person-centred and confidential professional support; and, finally, young people's confidence in the ability and suitability of specific professionals to deliver prevention sessions linked to their understanding of the key issues. This research identified the need to ensure that the right intervention is offered, at the right level, by the right person, as the consequences of providing the inappropriate 'sympathetic individual' can result in provision that appears to patronise, trivialise and alienate, rather than engage, young people. This also indicates the importance of co-producing teaching materials on these topics with young people and the need to continuously evaluate the impact of prevention programmes in schools.

The key issue identified was not focused on a gap in knowledge, lack of available support or unwillingness by the young women to access support if required, but rather on the lack of power of the young women to operationalise their knowledge as part of their intimate relationships. Therefore, prevention education needs to have a practical focus on providing young women with the ability to apply their understanding of relationship equality to their reality, while preparing young men to relinquish their power and privilege. Furthermore, the young women's narratives revealed a lack of understanding of what it means to operationalise equality in relationships in order to have equal power.

Despite potential limitations, this research contributes to the literature and prevailing debates on the nature of teenage intimate relationships and the themes of gendered expectations and social norms, sexism, the influence of social media, young people's understanding of abuse within their intimate relationships and their ideas of a healthy relationship. In doing so, it extends our knowledge of young women's attitudes towards gender, social norms and intimate relationships. The young women's narratives illustrated the challenge of shifting young men's power, due to the cultural attitudes that perpetuate established hierarchical gendered identities which favour men over women. Preparing young men to relinquish at least a portion of their power needs to be incorporated as part of prevention education. Prevention programmes geared towards empowering young women should focus on promoting their confidence and individual agency. This re-evaluation will assist young women to construct their position in a manner that reduces the likelihood that any form of negotiation and power comes at a cost. This cost, seen within their narratives, was the emotion work of the management of this power imbalance and the requirement to 'subtly' perform their expected girlfriend role, due to the lack of negotiating space within their intimate relationships. The gaps between young women's attitudes, their desires, expectations and their 'everyday' experiences draw attention to the complex dilemma for young women when performing their role in intimate relationships.

The findings from the questionnaire and the interviews diverge; however, the journey on both paths reveals an image of young women unable to draw on a narrative of choice in order to assert their voice, their individual needs or negotiate their predetermined relationship script. Overall, this outlines the limited interpersonal power held by young women. For example, Glain saw it as positive that she had modified her behaviour to become "subtle". This essentially meant that she managed her appearance, behaviour and her performance of self in a manner that was socially desirable. She did not see her need for subtlety as a hindrance, but rather as a necessary expectation of being a young woman seeking respect, subsequently qualifying her actions as "but I'm weird". It was apparent that young women lacked the power to operationalise their egalitarian attitudes in order to engage in relationships that adhere to the description of what they expect, want or desire within a 'healthy relationship'. As a default position, they relied and drew upon normative scripts focused on essentialist beliefs.

The future: recommendations for research, policy and practice

Research

- Future research should aim to create a space specifically for young men to share their attitudes and experiences of their intimate relationships. The focus should be on accessing a sample of young men in schools rather than targeting a sample who are seen as 'perpetrators'. The aim should be to explore the impact of gender norms on their role within their intimate relationships, the progression of their intimate relationships, their views of a healthy relationship and their views on a continuum of abusive behaviour.

- There is a current gap in the research identifying the attitudes towards and exploring the experiences of young women's intimate relationships within the youth justice system. Again, this research should explore the impact of gender norms on their role within their intimate relationships, the progression of their relationships, their views of a healthy relationship and their views on a continuum of abusive behaviour.

- There is a current gap in the research identifying the attitudes towards and exploring the attitudes of the intimate relationships of young people who are ill or who have a disability. Again, this research should explore the impact of gender norms on their role within their intimate relationships, the progression of their intimate relationships, their views of a healthy relationship and their views on a continuum of abusive behaviour. This study should also concentrate on the opportunities for these young people to 'date', have an intimate relationship and their access to sex and relationship education that is focused on healthy relationships rather than risk.

- Future research should also aim to explore the attitudes towards and experiences of love, desire and pleasure within young intimate relationships. There needs to be a greater focus on the power across the progression of these relationships.

- There needs to be a more intersectional approach to research with young people on this topic, in order to allow the space to explore the interactions of different positions on the nature of the progression of young people's relationships and any abuse suffered as part of these relationships.

- The design of future research in this area should be co-produced with an advisory group of young people who are representative of the research sample group.

- Future research in this area should focus on adopting a 'mixed-methods' approach to gather both the attitudes and experiences of young people.

- Research on young intimate relationships should include a specific emphasis on exploring the development and progression of these relationships, rather than a narrow focus on the abusive behaviour that may be experienced as part of these relationships. I would therefore suggest that the direction of future research with young women should focus on longitudinal research exploring the progression of their intimate relationships, with attention given to love, pleasure and desire.

Policy

- The development of a policy on 'healthy relationship' education should focus on a 'whole-community approach' that includes a focus on tackling gender norms as its foundation. This policy should go beyond the school setting in order to incorporate key multi-agency stakeholders, parents/carers and the wider community as a whole. The ethos of including young people and other key stakeholders to co-produce intervention tools to be used with young people should also be a key component of this policy.

Practice

- Abusive behaviour in teenage relationships was overtly displayed in schools, indicating a lack of awareness of acceptable behaviours. This reflects the fact that it has become acceptable among young people to display these types of behaviour in the public arena, reflecting their normalisation of verbal and emotional abuse. The visibility of this behaviour may not necessarily function as a protective factor, and requires specific consideration when designing prevention programmes.
- There were several barriers and enablers for young women when attempting to access support provision. The importance of privacy was crucial, as several young women noted that queuing for an appointment with the school nurse only served to raise questions and gossip (primarily around sex, in particular, contraception and unwanted pregnancies). The status of the professional was also important, as there was a general consensus that they would not access the school child protection lead, as this was often the deputy head. This was primarily due to their fear that the information would be shared and dealt with disproportionately, and due to their perception that this role was disengaged from the pupils.
- The young women wanted prevention interventions that empowered them to make informed choices and gave them the scripts to reject unwanted attention/requests, as they wanted to learn about "How to say 'no' to guys, no to sex, no to pictures" (Aleysha) and "Need to know about respect and keeping sex lives private" (Claire).
- There was a sense that young men's abusive behaviour was natural, and was justified as a response to provocation by their girlfriends. This raises two key points for the design of prevention education. Firstly, there is a need to challenge our understanding of young men and men's behaviour, gendered norms of femininity, masculinity, abuse, violence and aggression. Young people should receive education and support through the adoption of a gender lens, in order to understand how they use gender to naturalise, justify and excuse abusive behaviour. Secondly, there is a need to have structural and institutional responses focused on shaping youth mainstream cultures of gendered norms, rather than an individualistic approach concentrated on individual solutions and justifiable or expected behaviour. There needs to be a greater focus on developing spaces in order to enable

young women to develop their own sexual identities, including a re-focus on sexual desire, pleasure and love.

Final thoughts

In the UK, we are currently in a period of change, some of which has been planned as a result of the development of the Domestic Abuse Act 2021; some aspects of change, such as the impact of the COVID-19 pandemic, were unplanned and will continue to be so for years to come. Progress has been made in the form of raising awareness on the nature of abuse in young people's intimate relationships. Great gains have also been made in developing robust global evidence in order to understand the nature and impact of intimate relationship abuse and wider harassment on young women. Despite this, the space to give young women a voice to share their experiences continues to be limited. As a result, the nuanced details of their experiences can often be misunderstood or assumed by adults, either from a policy or on a practical basis. This reinforces the need to develop the ethos of routinely including young women specifically in policy, research and practice developments. Current gendered social norms establish the static role of being a young woman. This also influences the heteronormative ideas of young intimate relationships, which shape young women's space to influence change. To genuinely release the potential of young women, we need to deconstruct and re-focus the equitable power balance across society. The old normative scripts dictating the traditional powerless roles for young women can only change if the whole community gives them power, space and a real voice. We need to empower all young women to perform their chosen role, without fear of shame, stigma and social exclusion; only then can they truly remove their mask of performing the scripted 'ideal girlfriend role'.

Pen pictures:
interview participants

Participant	Age	School year	Area	Relationship status
Chloe	15 years old	Year 11	Rural	Chloe was in a relationship that lasted a year.
Michelle	16 years old	Year 11	Rural	Michelle had been in several relationships, but was currently single.
Becky	18 years old	Year 13	Rural and urban	Becky had been in several relationships. She is currently in a long-term relationship.
Glesni	17 years old	Year 12	Rural and urban	Glesni has been in a relationship. She is currently single, but is 'seeing' her ex- boyfriend.
Mali	16 years old	Year 11	Rural	Mali had been in two relationships. She is currently single.
Glain	15 years old	Year 10	Rural	Glain has not been in a relationship and has limited experience of 'going out' with boys.
Aleysha	16 years old	Year 11	Rural	Aleysha has had several boyfriends and is currently in a long-term relationship with an older boyfriend (19 years old).
Jennifer	18 years old	Year 13	Rural and urban	Jennifer has had several boyfriends and is currently in a long-term relationship with a boyfriend in her school year. Her wish is to bring this relationship to an end as soon as possible.
Elen	18 years old	Year 13	Rural and urban	Elen has had several boyfriends and is currently in a long-term relationship. She describes the impact of abuse experienced as part of a long-term relationship which has now ended.
Bonnie	18 years old	Not in education or employment. Working with the Youth Offending Service.	Rural	Bonnie has had several intimate relationships. She is currently in a long-term relationship with an older man (21 years old), who has a daughter. Bonnie does not live with her boyfriend, but she does

(continued)

Participant	Age	School year	Area	Relationship status
				stay with him at weekends. She has an acrimonious relationship with her boyfriend's ex-partner. She also describes the impact of abuse experienced with an ex-boyfriend who was the same age as her; she met him through the Youth Offending Service and described how he was in and out of custody.
Lowri	15 years old	Year 10	Rural	Lowri has had one significant relationship with a young man in her school year. She describes that he was emotionally abusive towards her. The relationship ended when her father intervened and refused to allow her to continue the relationship.
Rhiannon	18 years old	Year 13	Rural and urban	Rhiannon has been in several relationships. She is currently single.
Megan	15 years old	Year 10	Urban	Megan has not been in a relationship and has limited experience of 'going out' with boys.
Delyth	17 years old	Year 12	Rural and urban	Delyth has relationship experience. She is currently single.
Ceri	18 years old	Year 13	Rural and urban	Ceri has not been in a relationship and has limited experience of 'going out' with boys.
Claire	16 years old	Year 11	Rural	Claire is in a long-term relationship with her current boyfriend. This is her first serious relationship.
Diane	18 years old	Year 13	Urban and rural	Diane has not been in a relationship and has limited experience of 'going out' with boys.
Bella	16 years old	Year 11	Rural	Bella has been in one short-term relationship with a boy the same age as her. However, her parents disapproved and disallowed her from meeting up with him.
Collette	15 years old	Year 11	Rural	Collette has not been in a relationship and has limited experience of 'going out' with boys.
Julie	15 years old	Year 11	Rural	Julie has not been in a relationship and has limited experience of 'going out' with boys.
Mair	15 years old	Year 11	Urban and rural	Mair has not been in a relationship and has limited experience of 'going out' with boys.

Participant	Age	School year	Area	Relationship status
Margaret	15 years old	Year 11	Rural	Margaret has not been in a relationship and has limited experience of 'going out' with boys.
Grug	15 years old	Year 10	Rural	Grug has not been in a relationship and has limited experience of 'going out' with boys.
Alexis	16 years old	Year 11	Rural	Alexis has not been in a relationship and has limited experience of 'going out' with boys.
Donna	16 years old	Year 11	Rural	Donna has been in a long-term relationship for over two years with her current boyfriend. He is a year older than her.

Notes

Chapter 1

[1] I wanted to make clear that even though I'm a social worker, the relevant and usual safeguarding process would need to be followed, as with all other research, and a clear safeguarding protocol was established with both heads of education and all the participating schools. This meant that each school had a safeguarding lead for the project and each local authority area also had a senior safeguarding lead for the project in the event that anything was disclosed as part of the interviews that warranted a safeguarding response.

Chapter 3

[1] Tinder is a location-based dating app that allows users to communicate with each other.

Chapter 5

[1] Nudies is a term often used by young people when a request is received for a naked or partially naked photo. These requests are often sent via instant or text messaging. This practice is often linked to sexting.

[2] SpongeBob SquarePants is a cartoon character of a sponge who lives in a fictional underwater city.

Chapter 6

[1] The amendment to the Children and Social Work Bill 2017 will make relationship education in primary schools and relationship and sex education in secondary schools compulsory, with this timescale changing on several occasions in England. However, parents/carers will have the right to withdraw their child from this education provision.

[2] The Boys to Men project explored the reasons why some young men become perpetrators of domestic abuse, with a focus on looking into what can be done to prevent young men from becoming perpetrators. The methods adopted included an attitudes questionnaire, young people's focus groups and biographical interviews with 30 young men.

[3] The 'Bedroom' video clip raised questions around abuse within teenage intimate relationships, with a focus on consent, coercion, and physical and sexual violence.

[4] The campaign is supported by a specific website: www.disrespectnobody.co.uk

[5] This was a BBC film focusing on the real-life events of a young woman's violent and abusive relationship from the age of 17 years old until she was killed by her boyfriend at the age of 21.

References

Action Canada for Sexual Health and Rights (2019). Action Canada for Sexual Health and Rights [online]. Available from: actioncanadashr.org

Allen, L. (2008). 'They Think You Shouldn't Be Having Sex Anyway': Young People's Suggestions for Improving Sexuality Education Content. *Sexualities*, 11(5), 573–594.

Antle, B.F., Karam, E., Christensen, D.N., Barbee, A.P., and Bibhuti, K.S. (2011). An Evaluation of Healthy Relationship Education to Reduce Intimate Partner Violence. *Journal of Family Social Work*, 14, 387–406.

APPG for UN Women (2021). *Prevalence and Reporting of Sexual Harassment in UK Public Spaces* [online]. Available from: APPG-UN-Women-Sexual-Harassment-Report_Updated.pdf unwomenuk.org

Baker, C., and Carreño, P. (2016). Understanding the Role of Technology in Adolescent Dating and Dating Violence. *Journal of Child and Family Studies*, 25, 308–320.

Barter, C. (2016). *Interpersonal Violence and Abuse in Young People's Relationships: Frontline Briefing*. Dartington: Research in Practice.

Barter, C., McCarry, M., Berridge, D., and Evans, K. (2009). *Partner Exploitation and Violence in Teenage Intimate Relationships* [online]. Available from: www.womenssupportproject.co.uk/userfiles/file/partner_exploitation_and_violence_report_wdf70129.pdf

Barter, C., Stanley, N., Wood, M., Aghtaie, N., Larkins, C., Øverlien, C., and Lesta, S. (2015). *Safeguarding Teenage Intimate Relationships (STIR): Connecting Online and Offline Contexts and Risks. Research Report* [online]. Available from: http://stiritup.eu/wpcontent/uploads/2015/06/STIR-Exec-Summary-English.pdf

Bates, L. (2014). *Everyday Sexism*. London: Simon and Schuster UK.

Bates, S. (2017). Revenge Porn and Mental Health: A Qualitative Analysis of the Mental Health Effects of Revenge Porn on Female Survivors. *Feminist Criminology*, 12(1), 22–42.

Berelowitz, S., Firmin, C., Edwards, G., and Gulyurtlu, S. (2012). 'I Thought I Was the Only One. The Only One in the World'. The Office of the Children's Commissioner's Inquiry into Child Sexual Exploitation in Gangs and Groups [online]. Available from: www.childrenscommissioner.gov.uk/report/i-thought-i-was-the-only-one-in-the-world

Bogle, K.A. (2008). *Hooking Up: Sex, Dating, and Relationships on Campus*. New York: NYU Press.

Bond-Taylor, S., and Davies, C.T. (2020). Flexibility and Pedagogy, in Dennis, C., Abbott, S., Matheson, R., and Tangney, S. (eds). *Higher Education: Delivering Flexibility in Learning through Online Learning Communities*. Leiden: Brill, pp 97–108.

Borland, K. (1991). 'That's Not What I Said': Interpretive Conflict in Oral Narrative Research, in Gluck, S.E., and Patai, D. (eds). *Women's Words: The Feminist Practice of Oral History.* New York: Routledge, pp 63–76.

Boserup, B., McKenney, M., and Elkbuli, A. (2020). Alarming Trends in US Domestic Violence during the COVID-19 Pandemic. *The American Journal of Emergency Medicine,* 38(12), 2753–2755. https://doi.org/10.1016/j.ajem.2020.04.077

Boxall, H., Morgan, A., and Brown, R. (2020). *The Prevalence of Domestic Violence among Women during the COVID-19 Pandemic.* Statistical Bulletin No. 28. Canberra: Australian Institute of Criminology [online]. Available from: https://doi.org/10.52922/sb04718

Bronfenbrenner, U. (1979). *The Ecology of Human Development: Experiments by Nature and Design.* Cambridge, MA: Harvard University Press.

Burman, M., and Cartmel, F. (2005). *Young People's Attitude towards Gendered Violence.* Edinburgh: NHS Scotland [online]. Available from: www.equation.org.uk/Young-Peoples-Attitudes-Towards-Gendered-Violence

Burton, S., and Kitzinger, J., (1998). *Young People's Attitudes towards Violence, Sex and Relationships: A Survey and Focus Group Study* [online]. Available from: www.vawpreventionscotland.org.uk

CAADA (Co-ordinated Action Against Domestic Abuse) (2013). *CAADA Insights Factsheet: Teenage Victims of Domestic Violence* [online]. Available from: www.caada.org.uk/.../CAADA-insight-factsheet-teenage-domestic-abuse

Carver, K., Joyner, K., and Udry, J.R. (2003). National Estimates of Adolescent Romantic Relationships, in Florsheim, P. (ed). *Adolescent Romantic Relations and Sexual Behaviour: Theory, Research, and Practical Implications.* Mahwah, NJ: Lawrence Erlbaum, pp 23–56.

CDC (Centers for Disease Control and Prevention) (2018). *What Is Dating Matters?* [online]. Available from: www.cdc.gov/violenceprevention/intimatepartnerviolence/datingmatters/index.html

CDC (2021). *What Works: Sexual Health Education* [online]. Available from: www.cdc.gov/healthyyouth/whatworks/what-works-sexual-health-education.htm

Children's Commissioner for Wales (2013). *Annual Report 2012/13* [online]. Available from: www.childcom.org.uk/en/publications-list

Chung, D. (2005). Violence, Control, Romance and Gender Equality: Young Women and Heterosexual Relationships. *Women's Studies International Forum,* 28, 445–455.

Cislaghi, B., and Heise, L. (2018). Theory and Practice of Social Norms Interventions: Eight Common Pitfalls. *Global Health,* 14, 83. https://doi.org/10.1186/s12992-018-0398-x

Cislaghi, B., Manji, K., and Heise, L. (2018). *Social Norms and Gender Related Harmful Practices: What Assistance from the Theory to the Practice?* London: LSHTM [online]. Available from: https://doi.org/10.17037/PUBS.04646973

Connell, R.W. (1987). *Gender and Power*. Oxford: Blackwell Publishers.

Cordis Bright (2019). *What Works in Providing Whole System Approaches to Domestic Abuse?* [online]. Available from: www.cordisbright.co.uk/admin/resources/12-evidence-reviews-whole-systems-approach-to-da.pdf

Coy, M. (2013). Children, Childhood and Sexualised Popular Culture, in Wild, J., (ed). *Exploiting Childhood: How Fast Food, Material Obsession and Porn Culture Are Creating New Forms of Child Abuse*. London: Jessica Kingsley, pp149–161.

Coy, M., Kelly, L., Vera-Gray, F., Garner, M., and Kanyeredzi, A. (2016). From 'No Means No' to 'an Enthusiastic Yes': Changing the Discourse on Sexual Consent through Sex and Relationships Education, in Sundaram, V., and Sauntson, H. (eds). *Global Perspectives and Key Debates in Sex and Relationships Education: Addressing Issues of Gender, Sexuality, Plurality and Power*. London: Palgrave Pivot, pp84–99. https://doi.org/10.1057/9781137500229_6

Crenshaw, K. (1989). *Demarginalizing the Intersection of Race and Sex: A Black Feminist Critique of Antidiscrimination Doctrine, Feminist Theory and Antiracist Politics*. University of Chicago Legal Forum: Article 8 [online]. Available from: https://chicagounbound.uchicago.edu/uclf/vol1989/iss1

Daniels, E.A., and Zurbriggen, E.L. (2016). The Price of Sexy: Viewers' Perceptions of a Sexualized versus Nonsexualized Facebook Profile Photograph. *Psychology of Popular Media Culture*, 5(1), 2–14.

Davies, C.T. (2019). This is Abuse?: Young Women's Perspectives of What's 'OK' and 'Not OK' in their Intimate Relationships. *Journal of Family Violence*, 34, 479–491. https://doi.org/10.1007/s10896-019- 00038-2

Debnam, K.J., and Temple, J.R. (2021). Dating Matters and the Future of Teen Dating Violence Prevention. *Prevention Science*, 22, 187–192. https://doi.org/10.1007/s11121-020-01169-5

DeKeseredy, W.S., and Schwartz, M.D. (2016). Thinking Sociologically about Image-Based Sexual Abuse: The Contribution of Male Peer Support Theory. Sexualization, Media, and Society, 2(4), 1–8. https://doi.org/10.1177per cent2F2374623816684692

de Melker, S. (2015). *The Case for Starting Sex Education in Kindergarten* [online]. Available from: www.pbs.org/newshour/health/spring-fever

Deutsch, F.M. (2007). Undoing Gender. *Gender and Society*, 21(1), 106–127.

Dewar, E. (2015). Promoting Healthy Relationships through Peer-to-Peer Learning. *British Journal of School Nursing*, 10(6), 306–307.

Drouin, M., and Tobin, E. (2014). Unwanted but Consensual Sexting among Young Adults: Relations with Attachment and Sexual Motivations. *Computers in Human Behavior*, 31, 412–418.

Drouin, M., Ross, J., and Tobin, E. (2015). Sexting: A New, Digital Vehicle for Intimate Partner Aggression? *Computers in Human Behavior*, 50, 197–204.

Eliffe, R., Holt, S., and Øverlien, C. (2020). Hiding and Being Hidden: The Marginalisation of Children's Participation in Research and Practice Responses to Domestic Violence and Abuse. *Social Work and Social Sciences Review*, 18(1), 5–24.

Elliott, S. (2010). Parents' Constructions of Teen Sexuality: Sex Panics, Contradictory Discourses, and Social Inequality. *Symbolic Interaction*, 33(2), 191–212.

Epstein, D., and Johnson, R. (1998). *Schooling Sexualities*. Buckingham: Open University Press.

Estyn (2017). *A Review of Healthy Relationships Education* [online]. Available from: www.cardiff.ac.uk/__data/assets/pdf_file/0016/1030606/informing-the-future-of-the-sex-and-relationships-education-curriculum-in-wales-web.pdf

European Commission (2020). *Sexuality Education across the European Union: An Overview* [online]. Available from: file:///C:/Users/User/Downloads/KE-03-20-671-EN-Nper cent20(2).pdf

EVAWG (2021). *Violence against Women and Girls (VAWG) Strategy 2021 to 2024: Call for Evidence* [online]. Available from: www.gov.uk/governm ent/consultations/violence-against-women-and-girls-vawg-call-for-evide nce/violence-against-women-and-girls-vawg-strategy-2021-2024-call-for-evidence

Fine, G.A. (1993). The Sad Demise, Mysterious Disappearance, and Glorious Triumph of Symbolic Interactionism. *Annual Review of Sociology*, 19, 61–87.

Fine, M. (1988). Sexuality, Schooling, and Adolescent Females: The Missing Discourse of Desire. *Harvard Educational Review*, 58(1), 29–53.

Fisher, B.S., and Sloan, J.J. (2011). *The Dark Side of the Ivory Tower: Campus Crime as a Social Problem*. New York: Cambridge University Press.

Fisher, C.M., Waling, A., Kerr, L., Bellamy, R., Ezer, P., and Mikolajczak, G., et al (2019). *6th National Survey of Australian Secondary Students and Sexual Health 2018*. ARCSHS Monograph Series No. 113. Bundoora: Australian Research Centre in Sex, Health and Society, La Trobe University. DOI: 10.26181/5c80777f6c35e

Fjær, E.G., Pedersen, W., and Sandberg, S. (2015). 'I'm Not One of Those Girls': Boundary-Work and the Sexual Double Standard in a Liberal Hookup Context. *Gender and Society*, 29(6), 960–981.

Flood, M. (2009). The Harms of Pornography Exposure among Children and Young People. *Child Abuse Review*, 18(6), 384–400.

Flood, M.G., and Pease, B. (2009). Factors Influencing Attitudes to Violence against Women. *Trauma, Violence and Abuse*, 10(2), 125–142.

Foshee, V.A. (1996). Gender Differences in Adolescent Dating Abuse Prevalence, Types and Injuries. *Health Education Research*, 11, 275–286.

Foshee, V.A., Bauman, K.E., Ennett, S.T., Linder, G.F., Benefield, T., and Suchindran, C. (2004). Assessing the Long-Term Effects of the Safe Dates Program and a Booster in Preventing and Reducing Adolescent Dating Violence Victimization and Perpetration. *American Journal of Public Health*, 94(4), 619–624. https://doi.org/10.2105/ajph.94.4.619

Fox, C.L., Corr, M.L., Gadd, D., and Butler, I. (2013). Young Teenagers' Experience of Domestic Violence. *Journal of Youth Studies*, 174, 510–526. DOI: 10.1080/13676261.2013.780125.

Gadd, D., Corr, M.L., Fox, C., and Butler, I. (2014). This Is Abuse … or Is It? Domestic Abuse Perpetrators' Responses to Anti-Domestic Violence Publicity. *Crime, Media, Culture*, 10(1), 3–22. DOI: 10.1177/1741659013475462.

Gagnon, J., and Simon, W. (1973). *Sexual Conduct: The Social Sources of Human Sexuality*. Chicago: Aldine.

Girlguiding (2021). *Sexual Harassment – Support for Girls and Leaders* [online]. Available from: www.girlguiding.org.uk/girls-making-change/ways-to-take-action/past-actions-and-campaigns/campaign-to-end-sexual-harassment/sexual-harassment--and-where-to-get-support

Goffman, E. (1955). On Face-Work: An Analysis of Ritual Elements in Social Interaction. *Psychiatry: Journal of Interpersonal Relations*, 18(3), 213–231.

Goffman, E. (1959). *The Presentation of Self in Everyday Life*. New York: Anchor Books.

Goffman, E. (1963). *Stigma: Notes on the Management of Spoiled Identity*. Englewood Cliffs, NJ: Prentice-Hall.

Goffman, E. (1967). *Interaction Ritual: Essays on Face-to-Face Behavior*. New York: Anchor Books.

Goffman, E. (1971). *Relations in Public: Microstudies of the Public Order*. New York: Basic Books.

Goffman, E. (1974). *Frame Analysis: An Essay on the Organization of Experience*. New York: Harper and Row.

Goffman, E. (1977). The Arrangement between the Sexes. *Theory and Society*, 4(3), 301–332.

Goffman, E. (1983). The Interaction Order. *American Sociological Review*, 48(1), 1–17.

Hasinoff, A.A. (2015). *Sexting Panic: Rethinking Criminalization, Privacy, and Consent (Feminist Media Studies)*. Chicago, IL: University of Illinois Press.

Hellevik, P. (2017). Digital Intimate Partner Violence and Abuse among Youth: A Systematic Review of Associated Factors, in Holt, S., Øverlien, C., and Devaney, J. (eds). *Responding to Domestic Violence: Emerging Challenges for Policy, Practice and Research in Europe*. London and Philadelphia: Jessica Kingsley Publishers, pp 192–214.

Henry, N., Flynn, A., and Powell, A. (2020). Technology-Facilitated Domestic and Sexual Violence: A Review. *Violence against Women*, 26(15–16), 1828–1854. DOI: 10.1177/1077801219875821.

Hickman, L.J., Jaycox, L.H., and Aronoff, J. (2004). Dating Violence among Adolescents: Prevalence, Gender Distribution, and Prevention Program Effectiveness. *Trauma, Violence and Abuse*, 5(2), 123–142.

Hird, M.J., and Jackson, S. (2001). Where 'Angels' and 'Wusses' Fear to Tread: Sexual Coercion in Adolescent Dating Relationships. *Journal of Sociology*, 37(1), 27–43. DOI :10.1177/144078301128756184.

Home Office (2013). *New Definition of Domestic Violence and Abuse to Include 16 and 17 Years Olds* [online]. Available from: www.gov.uk/government/news/new-definition-of-domestic-violence-takes-effect

Home Office (2015). *This Is Abuse Summary Report* [online]. Available from: www.gov.uk/government/publications/this-is-abuse-summary-report

Home Office (2016). *Disrespect Nobody* [online]. Available from: www.disrespectnobody.co.uk/

HM Government (2016). *A Wole-system Multi-agency Approach to Serious Violence Preventions: A Resource for Local System Leaders in England* [online]. Available from: https://assets.publishing.service.gov.uk/government/uploads/system/uploads/attachment_data/file/862794/multi-agency_approach_to_serious_violence_prevention.pdf

HMIC (Her Majesty's Inspectorate of Constabulary) (2014). *Everyone's Business: Improving the Police Response to Domestic Abuse* [online]. Available from: www.justiceinspectorates.gov.uk/hmicfrs/wp-content/uploads/2014/04/improving-the-police-response-to-domestic-abuse.pdf

Hoadley, C. (2012). What Is a Community of Practice and How Can We Support It?, in Jonassen, D.H., and Land, S.M. (eds). *Theoretical Foundations of Learning Environments* (2nd edn), New York: Routledge, pp 287–300.

Horvath, M.A.H., Alys, L., Massey, K., Pina, A., Scally, M., and Adler, J.R. (2013). *'Basically … Porn Is Everywhere': A Rapid Evidence Assessment on the Effect that Access and Exposure to Pornography Has on Children and Young People* [online]. London: Office of the Children's Commissioner (OCC). Available from: www. childrenscommissioner.gov.uk/force_download. php?fp=per cent2Fclient_assetsper cent2Fcpper cent2Fpublicationper cent2F667per cent2FBasically_porn_is_everywhere_Final.pdf

Houghton, C. (2015). Young People's Perspectives on Participatory Ethics: Agency, Power and Impact in Domestic Abuse Research and Policy-Making. *Child Abuse Review*, 24(4), 235–248. https://doi.org/10.1002/car.2407

House of Commons Equality Committee (2016). *Sexual Harassment and Sexual Violence in Schools* [online]. Available from: www.parliament.uk/business/committees/committees-a-z/commons-select/women-and-equalities-committee/inquiries/parliament-2015/inquiry1

Humphreys, C., Houghton, C., and Ellis, J. (2008). *Literature Review: Better Outcomes for Children and Young People Experiencing Domestic Abuse – Directions for Good Practice* [online]. Available from: www.scotland.gov.uk/Publications/2008/08/04112612/13

Ipsos MORI (2017). *Online Abuse and Harassment: Ipsos MORI Survey for Amnesty International on Online Abuse and Harassment* [online]. Available from: www.ipsos.com/ipsos-mori/en-uk/online-abuse-and-harassment.

Jackson, S. (2005). 'Dear Girlfriend ...': Constructions of Sexual Health Problems and Sexual Identities in Letters to a Teenage Magazine. *Sexualities*, 8(3), 282–305.

Jackson, S., and Scott, S. (2010). *Theorizing Sexuality*. Maidenhead: Open University Press.

Jewkes, R., Flood, M., and Lang, J. (2014). From Working with Men and Boys to Changing Social Norms and Reducing Inequities in Gender Relations: A Paradigm Shift in Prevention of Violence against Women and Girls. *The Lancet*, 385(9977), 1580–1589.

Johansson, T., and Hammaren, N. (2007). Hegemonic Masculinity and Pornography: Young People's Attitudes toward and Relations to Pornography. *The Journal of Men's Studies*, 15(1), 57–70.

Kantor, L.M., and Lindberg, L. (2020). Pleasure and Sex Education: The Need for Broadening both Content and Measurement. *American Journal of Public Health*, 110(2), 145–148. https://doi.org/10.2105/AJPH.2019.305320

Kelly, L. (1988). *Surviving Sexual Violence*. Oxford: Basil Blackwell Ltd.

Kelly, L., Sharp, N., and Klein, R. (2014). *Finding the Costs of Freedom: How Women and Children Rebuild their Lives after Domestic Violence*. London: Solace Women's Aid.

Kimmel, M.S. (2002). 'Gender Symmetry' in Domestic Violence: A Substantive and Methodological Research Review. *Violence Against Women*, 8(11), 1332–1363.

Kirby, P. (2004). *A Guide to Actively Involving Young People in Research* [online]. Available from: www.invo.org.uk/posttypepublication/a-guide-to-activ ely-involving-young-people-in-research

Korkmaz, S. (2021). Youth Intimate Partner Violence: Barriers and Bridges during the Ending Process. *Journal of Gender-Based Violence*, 5(2), 183–197. DOI: 10.1332/239868021X16158344407215

Lacasse, A., and Mendelson, M.J. (2007). Sexual Coercion Among Adolescents: Victims and Perpetrators. *Journal of Interpersonal Violence*, 22(4), 424–437.

Lagerlöf, H., and Øverlien, C. (2022). School as a Context for Youth Intimate Partner Violence: Young Voices on Educational Sabotage. *Nordic Journal of Social Research*, 13(2), 1–15.

Lamont, E. (2014). Negotiating Courtship: Reconciling Egalitarian Ideals with Traditional Gender Norms. *Gender and Society*, 28(2), 189–211.

Lamont, E. (2020). *The Mating Game: How Gender Still Shapes How We Date*. Oakland, CA: University of California Press.

Lavoie, F., Robitaille, L., and Hébert, M. (2000). Teen Dating Relationships and Aggression: An Exploratory Study. *Violence against Women*, 6(1), 6–36.

Livingstone, S., Haddon, L., Görzig, A., and Ólafsson, K. (2010). *Risks and Safety for Children on the Internet: The UK Report* [online]. LSE, London: EU Kids Online. Available from: http://eprints.lse.ac.uk/33730

Lundy, L. (2007). Voice Is Not Enough: Conceptualising Article 12 of the United Nations Convention on the Rights of the Child. *British Educational Research Journal*, 33(6), 927–942.

Macdowall, W., Jones, K.G., Tanton, C., Clifton, S., Copas, A.J., and Mercer, C.M., et al (2015). Associations between Source of Information about Sex and Sexual Health Outcomes in Britain: Findings from the Third National Survey of Sexual Attitudes and Lifestyles (Natsal-3). *BMJ Open*, 5, e007837.

Mahoney, M.R. (1991). Legal Images of Battered Women: Redefining the Issue of Separation. *Michigan Law Review*, 90, 2–94.

Makepeace, J.M. (1981). Courtship Violence among College Students. *Family Relations*, 30(1), 97–102.

Martellozzo, E., Monaghan, A., Adler, J.R., Davidson, J., Leyva, R., and Horvath, M.A.H. (2016). *'... I Wasn't Sure It Was Normal to Watch It ...': A Quantitative and Qualitative Examination of the Impact of Online Pornography on the Values, Attitudes, Beliefs and Behaviours of Children and Young People* [online]. Available from: www.nspcc.org.uk/services-and-resources/research-and-resources/2016/i-wasnt-sure-it-was-normal-to-watch-it

Marwick, A., and Boyd, D. (2014). 'It's Just Drama': Teen Perspectives on Conflict and Aggression in a Networked Era. *Journal of Youth Studies*, 17(9), 1187–1204.

McCarry, M. (2012). Who Benefits? A Critical Reflection of Children and Young People's Participation in Sensitive Research. *International Journal of Social Research Methodology*, 15(1), 55–68.

McGlynn, C., and Rackley, E. (2017). Image-Based Sexual Abuse. *Oxford Journal of Legal Studies*, 37(3), 534–561.

McGlynn, C., Rackley, E., and Houghton, R. (2017). Beyond 'Revenge Porn': The Continuum of Image-Based Sexual Abuse. *Feminist Legal Studies*, 25(25), 25-46.

McLeod, D.A., Jones, R., and Cramer, E.P. (2015). An Evaluation of a School-based, Peer-Facilitated, Healthy Relationship Program for At-Risk Adolescents. *Children and Schools*, 37(2), 108–116.

McRobbie, A. (2007). Young Women and the Post-Feminist Sexual Contract. *Cultural Studies*, 21(4–5), 718–737.

Meier, A., and Allen, G. (2009). Romantic Relationships from Adolescence to Young Adulthood: Evidence from the National Longitudinal Study of Adolescent Health. *The Sociological Quarterly*, 50(2), 208–335.

Miner, K., Jayaratne, T., Pesonen, A., and Zurbrügg, L. (2012). Using Survey Research as a Quantitative Method for Feminist Social Change, in Hesse-Biber, S.N. *Handbook of Feminist Research: Theory and Praxis*. Thousand Oaks, CA: SAGE Publications, pp 237–263.

Molidor, C., and Tolman, R.M. (1998). Gender and Contextual Factors in Adolescent Dating Violence. *Violence against Women*, 4(2), 180–194.

Mullender, A., Hague, G.M., Imam, I., Kelly, L., Malos, E.M., and Regan, L. (2002). *Children's Perspectives on Domestic Violence*. London: SAGE Publications.

Nayak, A., and Kehily, M.J. (2008). *Gender, Youth and Culture: Young Masculinities and Femininities*. Basingstoke: Palgrave.

NCB (National Children's Bureau) (2016). *Sex and Relationships Education* [online]. Available from: www.ncb.org.uk/listing-tag/sex-and-relationships-education

Neale, B. (1999). *Post Divorce Childhoods* [online]. Available from: www.leeds.ac.uk/family

Nelson, S. and Baldwin, N. (2016). Community prevention of CSA: a model for practice in *Tackling Child Sexual Abuse*. Bristol, UK: Policy Press. Available from: https://bristoluniversitypressdigital.com/view/book/97814473138

Ng, L.L., and Pemberton, J. (2013). Research-Based Communities of Practice in UK Higher Education. *Studies in Higher Education*, 38(10), 1522–1539. https://doi.org/10.1080/03075079.2011.642348

NICE (National Institute for Health and Care Excellence) (2016). *Domestic Violence and Abuse: Quality Standard* [online]. Available from: www.nice.org.uk/guidance/qs116/resources/domestic-violence-and-abuse-pdf-75545301469381

NSPCC (National Society for the Prevention of Cruelty to Children) (2021). *Report Abuse in Education Helpline Receives Hundreds of Calls since Launching in April* [online]. Available from: www.nspcc.org.uk/about-us/news-opinion/2021/report-abuse-education-helpline

OECD (2015). The ABC of Gender Equality in Education: Aptitude, Behaviour, Confidence. PISA [online]. Paris: OECD Publishing. Available from: http://dx.doi.org/10.1787/9789264229945-en

OFSTED (2013). *Not Yet Good Enough: Personal, Social, Health and Economic Education in Schools* [online]. Available from: www.gov.uk/government/publications/not-yet-good-enough-personal-social-health-and-economic-education

OFSTED (2021). *Review of Sexual Abuse in Schools and Colleges* [online]. Available from: www.gov.uk/government/publications/review-of-sexual-abuse-in-schools-and-colleges

ONS (2021). *Crime in England and Wales: Year Ending March 2021* [online]. Available from: www.ons.gov.uk/peoplepopulationandcommunity/crimeandjustice/bulletins/crimeinenglandandwales/yearendingmarch2021#:~:text=Theper cent20policeper cent20recordedper cent205.4per cent20million,excludingper cent20fraudper cent20andper cent20computerper cent20misuse

Överlien, C. (2017). Do You Want to Do Some Arm Wrestling?': Children's Strategies when Experiencing Domestic Violence and the Meaning of Age. *Child and Family Social Work*, 22(2), 680–688.

Överlien, C., Hellevik, P., and Korkmaz, S. (2020). Young Women's Experiences of Intimate Partner Violence – Narratives of Control, Terror, and Resistance. *Journal of Family Violence*, 35, 803–814.

Palmer M.J., Clarke, L, Ploubidis G.B., and Wellings, K. (2019). Prevalence and Correlates of 'Sexual Competence' at First Heterosexual Intercourse among Young People in Britain. *BMJ Sexual and Reproductive*, 45, 127–137.

Patai, D. (1991). US Academics and Third World Women: Is Ethical Research Possible?, in Gluck, S.E., and Patai, D. (eds). *Women's Words: The Feminist Practice of Oral History*. New York: Routledge, pp 137–154.

Phippen, A. (2012). *Sexting: An Exploration of Practices, Attitudes and Influences*. London: NSPCC.

Phipps, A., and Young, I. (2015). 'Lad Culture' in Higher Education: Agency in the Sexualization Debates. *Sexualities*, 18(4), 459–479.

Planned Parenthood (2021). *What's the State of Sex Education in the U.S.?* [online]. Available from: www.plannedparenthood.org/learn/for-educat ors/whats-state-sex-education-us

Powell, A., and Webster, K. (2018). Cultures of Gendered Violence: An Integrative Review of Measures of Attitudinal Support for Violence against Women. *Australian and New Zealand Journal of Criminology*, 51(1), 40–57. DOI: 10.1177/0004865816675669.

Price E.L., and Byers, E.S. (1999). The Attitudes towards Dating Violence Scales: Development and Initial Validation. *Journal of Family Violence*, 14, 351–375.

Public Health England (2019). *Child Sexual Exploitation: How Public Health Can Support Prevention and Intervention* [online]. Available from: https:// assets.publishing.service.gov.uk/government/uploads/system/uploads/atta chment_data/file/793351/Child_sexual_exploitation_how_public_health_ can_support_prevention_and_intervention.pdf

Radford, L., Corral, S., Bradley, C., Fisher, H., Bassett, C., and Howat, N., with Collishaw, S. (2011). *The Maltreatment and Victimisation of Children in the UK: NSPCC Report on a National Survey of Young People's, Young Adults' and Caregivers' Experiences*. London: NSPCC.

Rattansi, A., and Phoenix, A. (1997). Rethinking Youth Identities: Modernist and Postmodernist Frameworks, in Bynner, J., Chisholm, L., and Furlong, A. (eds). *Youth, Citizenship and Social Change in a European Context*. Aldershot, UK: Ashgate, pp 121–150.

Refuge (no date). *Starting in School to End Domestic Violence* [online]. Available from: www.refuge.org.uk/files/starting-in-schools.pdf

Reinharz, S. (1992). *Feminist Methods in Social Research*. New York: Oxford University Press.

Renold, E. (2013). *Boys and Girls Speak Out: A Qualitative Study of Children's Gender and Sexual Cultures* (Age 10–12) [online]. Available from: www.nspcc.org.uk/globalassets/documents/research-reports/boys-girls-speak-out-report.pdf

Renold, E., and Barter, C. (2000). 'I Wanna Tell You a Story': Exploring the Application of Vignettes in Qualitative Research with Children and Young People. *International Journal of Social Research Methodology*, 3(4), 307–323. DOI: 10.1080/13645570050178594

Renold, E., and McGeeney, E. (2017). *Informing the Future of the Sex and Relationships Education Curriculum in Wales*, Project Report. Cardiff: Cardiff University.

Ringrose, J., and Renold, E. (2012). Teen Girls, Working-Class Femininity and Resistance: Retheorising Fantasy and Desire in Educational Contexts of Heterosexualised Violence. *International Journal of Inclusive Education*, 16(4), 461–477.

Ringrose, J., Gill, R., Livingstone, S., and Harvey, L. (2012). *A Qualitative Study of Children, Young People and 'Sexting': A Report Prepared for the NSPCC*. London: NSPCC.

Rivers, I., and Duncan, N. (2013). *Bullying: Experiences and Discourses of Sexuality and Gender*. London: Routledge.

Rosen, D. (2004). 'I Just Let Him Have his Way': Partner Violence in the Lives of Low-Income, Teenage Mothers. *Violence against Women*, 0(1), 6–28.

Ryle, R. (2017). *Questioning Gender: A Sociological Exploration* (3rd edn). London: Sage Publications.

SafeLives (2014). *SafeLives Dash Risk Checklist: Quick Start Guidance* [online]. Available from: www.safelives.org.uk/sites/default/files/resources/Dash per cent20riskper cent20checklistper cent20quickper cent20startper cent20guidanceper cent20FINAL_1.pdf

Schutt, N. (2006). *Domestic Violence in Adolescent Relationships: Young People in Southwark and their Experiences with Unhealthy Relationships* [online]. Available from: www.cassandralearningcentre.org.uk/wpcontent/uploads/2010/11/southwarkstudy.doc

Shaw, C., Brady, L.M., and Davey, C. (2011). *Guidelines for Research with Children and Young People*. London: NCB Research Centre, National Children's Bureau.

Sieg, E. (2000). So Tell Me What You Want, What You Really Really Want … New Women on Old Footings? *Feminism and Psychology*, 10(4), 498–503.

Smith, C., Bradbury-Jones, C., Lazenbatt, A., and Taylor, J. (2013). *Provision for Young People Who Have Displayed Harmful Sexual Behaviour* [online]. Available from: www.nspcc.org.uk/globalassets/documents/research-reports/provision-young-people-displayed-harmful-sexual-behaviour.pdf

Smith, J.E., Waldorf, A.V., and Trembath, D.L. (1990). Single White Male Looking for Thin, Very Attractive… *Sex Roles*, 23(11/12), 675–685.

Stanko, E.A. (1985). *Intimate Intrusions*. London: Unwin Hyman.

Stanley, N., Barter, C., Wood, M., Aghtaie, N., Larkins, C., Lanau, A., and Överlien, C. (2016). Pornography, Sexual Coercion and Abuse and Sexting in Young People's Intimate Relationships: A European Study. Journal of Interpersonal Violence, 33(19) 2919–2944. https://doi.org/10.1177per cent2F0886260516633204

Stark, E. (2007). *Coercive Control: How Men Entrap Women in Personal Life*. New York: Oxford University Press.

Stein, N., and Kadin, K.D. (2017). Do Schools Normalise Sexual Harassment? An Analysis of a Legal Case Regarding Sexual Harassment in a Swedish High School. *Gender and Education*, 31(7), 920–937. DOI: 10.1080/09540253.2017.1396292

Stonard, K., Bowen, E., Walker K., and Price, S.A. (2015). They'll Always Find a Way to Get to You: Technology Use in Adolescent Romantic Relationships and Its Role in Dating Violence and Abuse. *Journal of Interpersonal Violence*, 1–35. DOI: 10.1177/0886260515590787

Sundaram, V. (2014). 'You Can Try, but You Won't Stop It. It'll Always be There': Youth Perspectives on Violence and Prevention in Schools. *Journal of Interpersonal Violence*, 31(4), 652–676.

Sundaram, V., and Jackson, C. (2015*). Is Lad Culture a Problem in Higher Education?: Exploring the Perspectives of Staff Working in UK Universities. Society for Research into Higher Education* [online]. Available from: www.srhe.ac.uk/downloads/JacksonSundaramLadCulture.pdf

Tanton, C., Jones, K.G., Macdowall, W., Clifton, S., Mitchell, K.R., and Datta, J., et al (2015). Patterns and Trends in Sources of Information about Sex among Young People in Britain: Evidence from Three National Surveys of Sexual Attitudes and Lifestyles. *British Medical Journal Open*, 5, e007834.

Tolman, D.L. (2002). *Dilemmas of Desire*. Cambridge, MA: Harvard University Press.

Tolman, D.L., Davis, B.R., and Bowman, C.P. (2016). 'That's Just How It Is': A Gendered Analysis of Masculinity and Femininity Ideologies in Adolescent Girls' and Boys' Heterosexual Relationships. *Journal of Adolescent Research*, 31(1), 3–31.

Totten, M. (2003). Girlfriend Abuse as a Form of Masculinity Construction among Violent, Marginal Male Youth. *Men and Masculinities*, 6(1), 70–92.

UNESCO (2009). *International Technical Guidance on Sexuality Education: An Evidence-Informed Approach for Schools, Teachers and Health Educators* [online]. Paris: UNESCO. Available from: http://unesdoc.unesco. org/images/0018/001832/183281e.pdf

United Nations (2019). *Global Study of Homicide* [online]. Available from: www.unodc.org/documents/data-and-analysis/gsh/Booklet1.pdf

Walker, K., and Sleath, E. (2017). A Systematic Review of the Current Knowledge Regarding Revenge Pornography and Non-Consensual Sharing of Sexually Explicit Media. *Aggression and Violent Behavior*, 36, 9–24.

Watts, C., and Zimmerman, C. (2002). Violence against Women: Global Scope and Magnitude. *Lancet*, 359(9313), 1232–1237.

West, C., and Zimmerman, D. (1987). Doing Gender. *Gender and Society*, 1(2), 125–151.

WHO (2005). *Researching Violence against Women: A Practical Guide for Researchers and Activists* [online]. Available from: www.who.int/reproductivehealth/publications/violence/9241546476/en

WHO (2021). *Global, Regional and National Estimates for Intimate Partner Violence against Women and Global and Regional Estimates for Non-Partner Sexual Violence against Women* [online]. Available from: www.who.int/news/item/09-03-2021-devastatingly-pervasive-1-in-3-women-globally-experience-violence

Williamson, E. (2010). Living in the World of the Domestic Violence Perpetrator: Negotiating the Unreality of Coercive Control. *Violence Against Women*, 16(12), 1412–1423.

Wolfe, D.A., Wekerle, C., Reitzel-Jaffe, D., Grasley, C., Pittman, A., and McEachran, A. (1997). Interrupting the Cycle of Violence: Empowering Youth to Promote Healthy Relationships, in Wolfe, D., McMahon, R., and Peters, D. (eds). *Child Abuse: New Directions in Prevention and Treatment across the Lifespan*. Thousands Oaks, CA: SAGE Publications, pp 102–129.

Women's Aid (2017). *Women's Aid Responds to the Latest Domestic Abuse Report from the ONS* [online]. Available from: www.womensaid.org.uk/womens-aid-responds-ons-latest-domestic-abuse-report

Wood, M., Barter, C., and Berridge, D. (2011). *Standing on my Own Two Feet: Disadvantaged Teenagers, Intimate Partner Violence and Coercive Control* [online]. Available from: www.nspcc.org.uk/Inform/research/findings/standing_own_two_feet_wda84543.html

Wood, M., and Barter, C. (2015). Hopes and Fears: Teenage Mothers' Experiences of Intimate Partner Violence. *Children and Society*, 29(6), 558–568.

Wood, M., Barter, C., Stanley, N., Överlien, C. (2015). Images across Europe: The Sending and Receiving of Sexual Images (Sexting) and Associations with Intimate Partner Violence in Young People's Relationships. *Youth Services Review*, 59, 149–160.

Zero Tolerance (2014). *'He's the Stud and She's the Slut': Young People's Attitudes to Pornography, Sex and Relationships* [online]. Available from: www.zerotolerance.org.uk

Index

References to tables appear in **bold** type. References to notes show both the page number and the note number (130n1). Names followed by ★ indicate research participants.